RECIPES FOR THE ROCKIES

Recipes for the Rockies

SARA CLARK

PRUETT PUBLISHING COMPANY

Library of Congress Cataloging in Publication Data

Clark, Sara.
Recipes for the Rockies.

Rev. ed. of: The wonderful world of Colorado cooking. 1970.
Includes index.
1. Cookery. I. Clark, Sara. Wonderful world of Colorado cooking. II. Title.
TX652.C55 1985 641.59788 85-6503
ISBN 0-87108-669-7 (pbk.)

First Edition
1 2 3 4 5 6 7 8 9

Printed in the United States of America

Contents

Introduction

It is my sincere desire, in writing this cookbook, to help my readers toward a more creative and artistic approach in preparing and serving food. Even the most simple meal can be a joy if served attractively with the idea that YOU are the artist, presenting your talents—not expecting each and every production to be a masterpiece, but, as a true artist, always inspired to his best. I know of no other field where the possibilities are so great for one to achieve tremendous satisfaction so often.

When you consider how much time, in our day, is concerned with preparing and eating food, we are well advised to make it as full of pleasure as is possible. Anyone who can read can cook! Today's magazines are full of marvelous recipes and serving tips, bookstores have cookbooks dealing with every kind of food interest you might have—you need not look far for material. Plan ahead, organize your work, and "keep your cool." Do as much as is possible toward preparation before your guests (or family) arrive—this will leave you free to enjoy the time with them and without the last-minute, hurried feeling so many cooks experience.

As you progress through this book, I shall endeavor to give you my ideas of attitude and approach which, I hope, will allow you to work with a light and happy heart, knowing the end result will be a more pleasant mealtime. I am sure you will feel you are serving some of the most delicious dishes possible for the delight of your family and guests.

Since my husband and I came to Colorado in 1946 from Wisconsin—our native state—we became interested in wild game hunting and cooking. I hope you will find my chapter on Outdoor Cookery especially interesting.

In the pages that follow I will try to present recipes, all of which have been tested in my own kitchen. All ingredients are readily available in Colorado markets. Today's shopping is not much of a problem, however, and you should be able to find most items at your supermarket, wherever you live. If there is any ingredient where a substitution is acceptable, I will give it to you in a footnote.

Courage my friends! Now let us begin toward our new adventure—with Recipes for the Rockies.

A Word About the New Edition: Health and Nutrition

Today, with nutrition and diet being stressed as important keys to good health, it is wise to maintain low levels of salt, fat, and sugar in recipes. I have already reduced the amount of salt for many of the recipes found in this book; far less, in fact, than that called for in the original version. However, it may be that you will wish to reduce levels still further. The average daily requirement, all inclusive, is only one-quarter teaspoonful, an allowance you may wish to keep in mind.

Fat consumption should also be cut to a minumum, something that can be accomplished by removing visible fat from meat, broth, soup stock, etc. Using Teflon pans and spray coating is also helpful in reducing fat content.

This new edition has been expanded to include a section of recipes for health and nutrition. However, I have tried not to cater to any specific diet, only to offer the most healthful, attractive, and tasty recipes possible from years of testing and compiling.

Here are a few newer recipes from my files and kitchen that I hope will bring you pleasure as well as good health.

Happy Cooking!

APPETIZERS

Actually, the appetizer for today's meals is usually served at cocktail time as a "finger-food," but whether or not this is your preference, it should set the stage for the main performance. What you serve may be elaborate or very simple, but it should not be so filling that it dulls the appetite for the meal to follow. Appetizer time is time for good conversation and sharing of interests, so keep it gay so that your meal can be enjoyed in complete harmony.

Let me take just a few moments to share with you something I think makes a "fun thing" out of serving appetizers—letting your family and/or guests cook their own on a cocktail hibachi (available at hardware and many specialty shops). It is a small Oriental grill and takes only three or four charcoal bricketts to make a good fire and can be used in any cooking area with no smoke from the cooking. Allow the coals to burn down to a nice glow thru powdered ash, outdoors, then bring indoors, if desired, and let everyone cook for himself. Previously prepare all the appetizers to the cooking stage, and the rest is easy!

Rumaki

I lb. chicken livers
I lb. bacon
¼ C. soy sauce
3 T. saki wine (optional)
½ t. fresh ginger root, grated OR
½ t. dry ginger

Pour boiling water over chicken livers, let stand 5 minutes. Drain. Combine soy sauce, saki, and ginger and pour over livers and allow to stand one hour. Meanwhile, precook bacon to partially remove the fat but do not crisp it. Remove livers from the marinade and wrap one-half strip bacon around a walnut-size piece of chicken liver. Secure with a bamboo skewer (these do not burn readily). Let each person grill his own on the hibachi, according to the desired doneness. This amount makes from 16 to 20 appetizers. You can figure about two per person.

Lobster Rumaki

1 pkg. (9 oz.) frozen small lobster tails, thawed
2 T. salad oil
¼ C. soy sauce
¼ C. dry sherry (optional)
1 t. grated lemon peel
10 slices bacon

Remove the shells from the lobster tails by cutting the soft undershell with a kitchen shears and pull meat out in one chunk. Cut into one-inch sections. Combine the oil, soy sauce, wine and lemon peel and pour over lobster pieces. Precook bacon, but do not allow it to become crisp. While slightly underdone, drain on a paper towel. Cut each slice in half and wrap around lobster pieces. Secure with bamboo skewers and allow each person to broil his own, over the hibachi, until bacon is crisp and lobster becomes firm and white (indicating it is done). Dunk in the following dip if desired:

1 7-oz. bottle low-calorie French dressing
2 t. cornstarch
½ C. water

Combine and cook over low heat until slightly thickened. Do not chill to serve.

When using your hibachi, explore the many possibilities by using such things as *cocktail sausages* or *smoked oysters* which have been rinsed with hot water and drained. A good dip for either of the above-mentioned is:

2/3 C. tomato catsup
2 t. lemon juice
1 t. grated onion
1 t. horseradish

Combine all ingredients. Let stand at room temperature one hour. The sausage and oysters need only to be heated through.

Cocktail Meatballs

1 lb. ground chuck
1 egg, beaten
½ C. fine, dry bread crumbs
1 t. salt
⅛ t. pepper
¼ t. garlic powder
2 T. Parmesan cheese

Combine all ingredients and form into bite-size balls.

In a heavy saucepan, combine 2 T. salad oil and 1 sliced clove garlic. Saute over low heat until garlic is limp but not brown. Remove garlic and add the meatballs to remaining fat—shake pan often to prevent meatballs from sticking. Brown balls lightly and remove from pan. Remove all but 1 T. fat from pan and add:

1 C. Dr. Pepper
¼ t. dry mustard
2 T. catsup
1 T. vinegar
1 T. soy sauce
Dash pepper

Bring to a boil and simmer 5 minutes. Add meatballs to sauce and allow to cook until most of liquid is absorbed—about 30 minutes. Makes 40 cocktail-size meatballs. Serve in a chafing dish or covered, small casserole with hors d' oeuvres picks.

The following recipe not only makes a fine appetizer, but is great for picnics or camping trips.

Pink Pickled Eggs With Beets

12 hard cooked eggs
1 large onion, sliced thin
1 C. cider vinegar
¼ C. sugar
1 t. salt
⅛ t. ground cloves
1 clove garlic
Fresh ground pepper to taste
2 1-lb. cans small whole beets

Drain the beets and reserve 1 C. of the beet juice. In a saucepan, combine beet juice with the vinegar, sugar, salt, cloves, garlic, and pepper, and bring to a boil and simmer 10 minutes.

Shell eggs and place in alternate layers, in a large jar or crock, with the sliced onions and beets. Pour the hot liquid over all. Stir occasionally as they cool. Refrigerate at least two days before using, stirring every day to encourage even coloring of eggs. Cut each egg in two, lengthwise, for serving as an appetizer. Dust with a bit of paprika and serve on a nest of parsley.

These are delightful either as an appetizer or as an accompaniment to steak or other meats.

Stuffed Mushrooms

12 large mushroom caps
4 T. butter
1 clove garlic, crushed
½ t. worchestershire sauce
¼ C. finely minced crab, lobster, or chicken*
1 egg, beaten
¼ C. fine dry bread crumbs
Melted butter
Parmesan cheese

Peel the mushroom caps and remove the stems. Wash stems, trim, and chop fine. Saute the caps in a heavy frying pan for a moment or two to coat well with butter. Remove to a shallow baking dish, hollow side up.

In remaining fat, saute the garlic and the chopped mushroom stems for 5 minutes. All the worchestershire sauce, soft crumbs, and minced crab, toss lightly.

Remove from heat and add the beaten egg and a light dash of salt. Heap the caps with this mixture, sprinkle with dry crumbs and brush with melted butter. Dust with a bit of Parmesan cheese. Bake at 350 degrees for 15 minutes. If caps are very large, they can be cut in two for serving on picks.

*Boned canned chicken may be used with good results.

Here is one that my gourmet friends say "If you haven't tried it, don't knock it!"

Steak Tartare

2 lbs. lean ground steak
2 eggs
½ C. finely minced onion
2 t. salt
Freshly ground black pepper
Cocktail Rye Bread, sliced thin

All fat and membrane must be removed from the meat before grinding, so either grind it yourself or instruct your butcher. The secret is to have perfect red meat. Combine meat and all ingredients except the rye bread and place in a chilled bowl surrounded by the unbuttered rye bread slices. Serve raw.

Pickled Mushrooms

2 pts. fresh mushrooms, washed & trimmed
1 med. onion, sliced into rings

Combine:
2/3 C. tarragon vinegar
½ C. salad oil
1 clove garlic, crushed
1 T. sugar
2 T. water
1 t. salt
Freshly ground black pepper

Pour this marinade over the mushrooms and onions. Cover and refrigerate over night, stirring several times. Drain and serve on picks.

These may be made ahead and kept frozen until ready to bake.

Cheese Puffs

1 C. grated sharp Cheddar Cheese
¼ C. soft butter
¼ C. sifted flour
¼ t. salt
½ t. paprika
24 pimento-stuffed green olives

Blend cheese and butter with a fork. Add flour, salt and paprika and mix well. Wrap about one teaspoonful of the mixture around each olive. Place on a baking sheet and freeze til firm—they can then be transferred to a plastic bag for storage in freezer. When ready to use, bake at 400 degrees for about 20 minutes or until delicately brown. Makes 24 puffs.

A perfect, big grapefruit or a pineapple with nice leaves at the top makes a fine base for fresh vegetable appetizers. (Use small cauliflowerettes, radishes, carrot slices, olives, and pickles.) Just impale the vegetables on picks and press into the grapefruit or pineapple. Serve with a dip of 1 C. sour cream, 1 T. grated onion, and 1 avocado, mashed, along with a dash of salt.

Wisconsin Cheese Log

Grate ¼ lbs. sharp Cheddar Cheese

Grate ½ C. unblanched almonds (to grate almonds, whirl in a blender)

Mix with:

1 8-oz. pkg. cream cheese

1 T. minced, canned pimento

¼ t. garlic salt

⅛ t. pepper

Mix all ingredients well and shape into a 1½-inch roll. Sprinkle a rectangle of waxed paper with paprika and roll the cheese "logj" up in the paper. Refrigerate several hours until firm. Serve in slices on crisp crackers.

Here's a little different treatment of an old standby:

Cracky Snacks

1 C. butter (2 sticks), melted
2 T. worchestershire sauce
1 clove garlic, crushed
1 t. salt
1 t. curry powder
½ t. tabasco sauce
2 pkg. (6¼ oz) corn chips
1 10-oz. can coconut chips
1 6-oz. pkg. cheese crackers
1 qt. Rice Chex
2 C. Cheerios
1 8-oz. small pretzel sticks
1 6-oz. can pecans
1 7½-oz. jar dry roasted peanuts

Add the worchestershire sauce, garlic, salt, curry powder and tabasco sauce to the melted butter and pour over the cereal and nut mixture in a large pan, stirring gently as you pour. Blend well. Turn onto cookie sheets and bake at 200 degrees F. for about 1½ hours. Stir frequently. Makes about 4 quarts.

Ham Puffs

Combine:
1 can deviled ham
1 egg yolk, poached and sieved
1 t. prepared mustard
¼ C. mayonnaise
1 t. grated onion
Fold in 1 stiffly beaten egg white.

Put a teaspoonful of this mixture on square saltine crackers. Sprinkle with a bit of grated Cheddar Cheese and broil 3 inches from the heat until puffed and brown. *Watch carefully!*

Savory Walnuts

In 4 T. hot butter, place 1 lb. shelled walnuts. Saute until well coated with butter. Add 2 t. worchestershire sauce, ½ t. salt, ⅛ t. pepper, and a dash of tabasco sauce. Place in a shallow baking pan and bake 20 minutes at 325 degrees F. Yield—4 cups.

Gourmet Shrimp

3 T. salad oil
1 lb. shrimp, frozen, shelled and deveined
3 T. finely chopped green onion
2 T. finely chopped candied ginger
1 clove garlic, crushed
3 T. chili sauce
1 T. catsup
3 T. dry white wine
1½ T. soy sauce
1 t. sugar
½ t. salt
¼ t. crushed red pepper

Thaw the shrimp and place in a fry pan with the salad oil. Stir and fry about 5 minutes until shrimp turns pink. Combine the remaining ingredients and pour over the shrimp. Stir rapidly for 1 minute. Serve on picks. Your guests will rave about this one!

Dips

The variety of dips is endless and I will only try to give you a few that are unusual.

Chili Con Queso (Chili Peppers with Cheese)

1 2-lb. box Velveeta Cheese, cut up
2 cans med. hot chili peppers (green)
1 large tomato, diced
1 small onion, minced
½ t. oregano
1 T. worchestershire sauce
2 cloves garlic, crushed
¼ t. salt
⅛ t. pepper

Combine all ingredients in the top of a double boiler and heat over simmering water until cheese melts and mixture is hot. Pour into a chafing dish and serve hot with large-size corn chips.

South-Of-The-Border Dip

1 15½-oz. can refried beans
½ C. sour cream
½ C. onion, finely minced
1½ T. worchestershire sauce
2 T. catsup or chili sauce
1 t. salt
¼ t. garlic powder
Dash of tabasco sauce

Combine all ingredients and serve in a bowl. Surround with corn chips.

Avocado Dip

3 large avocados, peeled and diced
1 8-oz. pkg. cream cheese, softened
½ t. salt
¼ C. mayonnaise
1 T. grated horseradish
2 T. grated onion
1 T. lemon juice

Place the ingredients in a mixing bowl and beat with electric mixer until smooth. This is a marvelous dip with fresh vegetables, cooked shrimp or lobster chunks, *cooked!* (Shrimp or lobster may be simmered in "Crab and Shrimp Spice" according to package directions. Do not overcook either the shrimp or lobster.)

Crab Dip

Rub a wooden bowl with a cut clove of garlic. Remove garlic clove and in the bowl place the following ingredients:

1 8-oz. pkg. cream cheese
2 t. lemon juice
1½ t. worchestershire sauce
½ t. salt
Dash of tabasco sauce
1 6-oz. can crab meat, minced fine

Mix well and thin slightly with a bit of milk. Serve as a spread for crackers or thinned to consistency for dipping potato chips.

This recipe is a bit of trouble to concoct, but it will please you with the end result.

Frosted Liver Pate

1 lb. chicken livers

½ lb. fresh mushrooms, washed & trimmed

¼ lb. butter

¾ t. salt

1 bunch green onions, chopped

4 hard cooked eggs, minced fine

Saute the chicken livers in the butter about 10 minutes. Add the onions and salt, cook 2 minutes and add the mushrooms which have been sliced. Cook 5 minutes. Put this mixture into a blender and whirl until smooth, adding a *small* amount of salad oil to keep the blades moving freely. Add the eggs but do not run in the blender—mix thoroughly and place mixture in a small, oiled bowl or mold. Chill thoroughly and remove from mold onto a chilled plate, round side up. In the meantime, prepare the "frosting":

Combine:

1 8-oz. package cream cheese

1 T. milk

and frost the pate generously. Decorate with sliced black olives and pimento. Serve surrounded by crisp crackers.

Here are two appetizers to be served at the table—the first is a version of a cold soup called Gazpacho, served in Mexico. Most delicious served the Mexican way or this American style:

Tangy Tomato Treat

1 pkg. vegetable flavored gelatin
1 C. boiling water
1 C. tomato juice
2 T. cider vinegar
1 med. green pepper, seeded and minced
½ C. sliced radishes
½ C. grated carrot
1 T. onion juice

Dissolve gelatin in hot water, add tomato juice and vinegar. Chill until mixture begins to thicken. Fold in the vegetables. Chill two or three hours, until set. Spoon into glasses or small glass cups. Garnish with a dollop of sour cream and a lemon slice for an extra flourish.

Avocado-Louis Appetizer

1 C. unflavored yogurt
¼ C. chili sauce
1 T. vinegar
1 t. grated onion
1 t. worchestershire sauce
½ t. salt
2 hard-cooked eggs
2 large avocados

Gently stir together the yogurt, chili sauce, onion, vinegar, worchestershire sauce, and salt. Blend well and chill. When you are ready to serve, cut the avocados, with a small melon baller or with a sharp measuring spoon, into small balls. Chop the eggs. Divide the yogurt mixture into six chilled glass bowls and surround with avocado balls. Sprinkle with chopped eggs for garnish.

Brie Cheese in Pastry (Elegant and So Easy)

Defrost *one* patty shell from a package (of 6) Pepperidge Farm party shells. Roll into a 5- or 6-inch round.

Remove packaging from a 4½-oz. package of Danish Brie cheese. Wrap the cheese completely in the pastry. Place seam-side down on an ungreased cookie sheet (do not prick pastry).

Bake at 400 degrees for 10 minutes. Reduce heat to 325 degrees and bake 5 to 7 minutes longer, until pastry is puffed and golden brown.

Cool 10 minutes before serving in small wedges. (Crust will be crunchy and the cheese soft and luscious.)

Serves 4 to 6.

BREAD, ROLLS, & PANCAKES

Best Herb Bread

Combine:
1 C. lukewarm milk
2 T. sugar
1 t. salt
1 beaten egg
1 pkg. instant dry yeast

Stir in:
1 C. flour
1 t. dry sage
2 t. caraway seeds
½ t. nutmeg

Beat vigorously and add:
2 T. soft butter
Flour

Beat well again and add enough more flour, a small amount at a time, until you can handle the dough with your hands. Dough must remain soft! Knead on a lightly floured board about 8 to 10 minutes, adding only enough flour to keep it from sticking.

Allow dough to rise to double its bulk. Divide dough in two and shape into two small loaves and place in well-oiled loaf pans 4 x 7⅝ inches or 1 large loaf. Allow to rise again to double its size. Bake small loaves at 375 degrees F. for 25 minutes or large loaf at 375 degrees F. for 40 to 45 minutes. Tap pan on bottom; if it sounds hollow, the bread is done. Butter the tops lightly while hot.

Mrs. Hoover's Oatmeal Bread

Pour 2 C. boiling water over 2 C. quick cooking oatmeal. Let stand ½ hour.

Add:
½ C. molasses
½ t. salt
1 T. soft shortening
1 cake compressed yeast softened in:
½ C. warm water
1 t. sugar
4 to 5 C. flour

(Add only half of the flour to the mixture, as flours differ and dough must be easy to handle without being too stiff!) Knead about 10 minutes, adding only the amount of flour necessary to keep dough from sticking to board. This will be a soft dough. Let rise to double its bulk, covered with a damp cloth. Divide into two loaves and let rise again to double its bulk. Bake at 325 degrees for 45 to 50 minutes.

This is a moist, delicious bread for cheese sandwiches.

Nothing perfumes the air like fresh bread baking.

Velma's Brown Bread

Sift together:
2 C. flour
1 C. cornmeal
½ t. soda
1 t. salt

Add:
2 C. sour or buttermilk
¾ C. molasses
½ C. chopped dates or raisins
½ C. chopped walnuts

Stir until all dry ingredients are well moistened. Fill 2 1-lb. coffee cans two-thirds full of the mixture. Cover with foil and steam 1½ hours.

NOTE: An improvised steamer may be made from a roasting pan with crumpled foil on the bottom. Put an inch or so of water in bottom of pan and settle your pans, with mixture to be steamed, firmly on the foil, but not touching pan. Cover tightly.

Corn Bread

1 C. flour, sifted
1 C. cornmeal
¼ C. sugar
3 t. baking powder
1 t. salt
1 egg, beaten
1 C. milk
4 T. melted shortening

Mix ingredients in order given. Bake at 400 degrees F. for 25 minutes in a 9 x 13 inch pan.

Zeta's Date Loaf (Sweet Bread)

Pour 2 C. boiling water over:
1½ C. pitted, diced dates

Add:
1 T. butter, melted
1¼ C. sugar
1 egg, beaten

Sift together:
2¾ C. flour, sifted
½ t. baking powder
2 t. soda
¼ t. salt
½ C. walnuts or pecans, chopped

Add the dry ingredients and the nuts to the date mixture and stir until well blended. Divide batter between two greased loaf tins and bake at 350 degrees for 45 to 50 minutes.

Ruth's Cowboy Cake (Coffee Cake)

Combine the following ingredients in a large bowl and rub with fingertips until like fine crumbs:

2½ C. sifted flour
2 C. brown sugar
½ t. salt
2/3 C. butter
2 t. baking powder
½ t. soda
½ t. cinnamon
½ t. nutmeg

Remove ½ C. of the above mixture and reserve for coffee cake topping. To the remainder add:

1 C. buttermilk
2 eggs, beaten

Divide between two greased layer cake pans and sprinkle each with some of the topping mixture. Bake at 375 degrees for 15 to 20 minutes.

Quick Apple Coffee Cake

2 C. flour, sifted
2 t. baking powder
1 t. salt
1 t. cinnamon
½ C. sugar
1 egg, beaten
¾ C. milk
1/3 C. melted butter
1 T. grated orange rind
3 apples, peeled and sliced

Combine the flour, baking powder, salt, cinnamon and sugar and sift into a bowl. Add the remaining ingredients except the apples. Stir batter until smooth and spread into a well-buttered square cake pan. Arrange the apple slices over the dough, pressing in gently. Sprinkle the apples with mixture of:

3 T. brown sugar
½ C. cinnamon
1 T. melted butter

Bake at 400 degrees about 25 minutes or until firm and apples are tender.

Want to impress the bridge club? Try:

Jim Jam Braid

(Using packaged roll mix)

1 pkg. hot roll mix, prepared according to the directions on package.

While dough rises, combine:

1 C. strawberry jam
½ C. finely cut dried apricots
½ C. finely chopped walnuts

Roll dough out into a rectangle 14 x 8 inches. Cut through dough, on the 14-inch side, at 1-inch intervals, up to within 3 inches of center. Spread filling down center of dough and lap the strips over the filling in a braiding fashion. Let rise to double its bulk, brush with 1 T. melted butter and sprinkle with 2 T. sugar. Bake at 350 degrees for 20 minutes until golden brown.

Southern Buttermilk Biscuits

Sift together:
3 C. flour, sifted
½ t. soda
3 t. baking powder
½ t. salt

Cut in ½ C. shortening
Slowly add:
1¼ C. Buttermilk

Stir gently and turn out on a lightly floured board. Roll or pat to thickness of ½ inch. Cut with a round cutter dipped in flour, lightly! Bake at 425 degrees for 15 minutes.

For crusty sides, place an inch apart to bake. For soft, fluffy biscuits, place close together.

Sis's Cinnamon Coffee Cake

Cream ½ C. butter and 1 C. sugar (*minus 2 T.*) until light and fluffy. Add 2 eggs, one at a time, beating well after each addition. Blend in 1 t. vanilla and ¼ t. lemon juice.

Sift together:
2 C. flour, sifted
1 t. soda
¾ t. baking powder

Add to the above butter and sugar mixture, *alternately* with the following

1 C. plus 2 T. sour cream
1 T. water

Ending with dry ingredients.

In a small bowl combine:
¼ C. brown sugar, firmly packed
2 T. granulated sugar
1½ t. cinnamon
¼ C. walnuts, chopped

Generously grease a 10-inch tube pan or scalloped 7-cup tube pan (Bundt pan). Spoon half the batter into pan, sprinkle with sugar and cinnamon mixture, spoon on remainder of batter, spreading evenly.

Bake at 350 degrees F. about 50 minutes to 1 hour or until a wooden pick inserted in center comes out clean. Cool on a rack, 10 minutes. Run a sharp knife around to and invert carefully on rack. Serve warm or cold.

Sourdough Bread

Starter batter: In a glass or pottery bowl (never use metal) combine:

2½ C. lukewarm water
1 pkg. dry yeast
2 C. flour, unsifted
1 T. sugar
1 t. salt

Combine and beat smooth. Let stand at room temperature, covered, for three or four days to develop the true "sourdough" flavor. Stir occasionally. Before using in a recipe, always remove some of the "sponge" (about a cupful) and put in a jar with a glass top, for use in making your next starter. Store in the refrigerator.

The bread:

Sprinkle 1 pkg. dry yeast over 1½ C. lukewarm water Add:

1 C. starter batter
2 t. sugar
1 t. salt

Blend well and add 2½ C. sifted flour. Beat well. Cover. Allow to rise to double its bulk.

Mix ½ t. soda with 1 C. sifted flour and stir into dough. Add only enough *more* flour to make dough easy to knead. (Keep dough soft and smooth!) Knead about 8 to 10 minutes. Shape in one large loaf on a cookie sheet, slash top, diagonally, several times. Let dough rise double and bake at 400 degrees for about 40 minutes or until golden brown. Brush top with melted butter. (When bread is thumped on the bottom, it should sound hollow.)

Sour Dough Pancakes

To 1 C. starter (see sourdough bread) add:

2 C. milk or water
2 C. flour

and mix well. Let stand, covered, in a warm place overnight. In the morning: (Reserve at least a cup of this mixture to put back in your "sourdough jar.") To what remains in the bowl, add:

1 egg
½ t. soda
½ t. salt
1 T. sugar
2 T. melted shortening

Mix well and bake on a hot griddle until golden brown on each side. Serve with maple syrup or sorghum.

Queen of Muffins

Cream together ¼ C. butter and 1/3 C. sugar. Add 1 egg, well beaten.

Sift together:
1½ C. flour
2 t. baking powder
½ t. salt

Add the dry ingredients alternately to the sugar and butter, with:

½ C. milk

Mix only until well blended. Bake in muffin pans, lined with paper baking cups, at 400 degrees for 15 to 18 minutes. Makes 12 muffins.

For variation: Add ¾ C. blueberries; ¾ C. mixed dates and walnuts; or ¾ C. cooked crisp bacon pieces.

Southern Grits Bread

½ C. hominy grits (cereal)
2 C. cold milk

Put hominy grits in the milk and place on medium heat, stirring constantly. Cook until thick. Add:

1 t. butter
½ t. salt
½ of an 8-oz. stick of smoky cheese
⅛ t. garlic powder
1 egg, beaten

Mix well and bake in a 9-inch casserole, greased well with butter, in a 400-degree oven for 30 minutes or until bread rises and top is nicely browned. Serve with butter.

Any leftover portion may be sliced and fried for breakfast!

Rice Griddlecakes

Sift:
1 C. flour with ¾ t. soda

Add:
1 C. leftover cooked rice
1 egg, beaten
1½ C. sour cream
2 T. melted butter
1 t. salt

Stir until well blended. Brown cakes on a hot griddle. Serve with honey or blueberry syrup.

Serve these with warm applesauce and well-browned sausages!

Potato Pancakes

Put 4 eggs in your blender, cover and beat until fluffy. Stop blender.

Add:
2/3 C. sifted flour
1 t. salt
2 T. salad oil
½ C. milk
1 T. onion, diced
2 C. pared, diced raw potatoes

Blend about 10 seconds, until smooth. Bake pancakes on hot griddle about 3 minutes on each side. Turn once. Serve with warm applesauce and butter!

CAKES & FROSTINGS

The crowning glory of your meal can be one of these delectable cakes. When you serve a rich cake, try to keep the meal reasonably simple.

Calla Lillies

Beat 3 eggs, slightly, and add:

1 C. sugar (less 2 T. sugar for about 5000 feet)
2 T. cold water
1 C. flour, sifted with:
1 t. baking powder
¼ t. salt

Beat 3 minutes. Drop by tablespoonfuls onto a greased and floured cookie sheet at 325 degrees for 8 to 10 minutes or until very *light* brown. While warm, roll each in shape of a cornucopia; secure with a string until cool. When ready to serve, fill with sweetened, whipped cream. Add powdered sugar to one egg yolk until stiff. Use a little to form the stamen on your Calla Lilly. Beautiful!

Date-Applesauce Cake

Sift together:
2 C. flour, sifted
2 t. soda
1 t. cinnamon
½ t. allspice
½ t. nutmeg
¼ t. cloves
¼ t. salt

Add:
2 eggs
1 C. brown sugar
½ C. butter, softened
1 C. applesauce

Beat 2 or 3 minutes until smooth. Add an additional 1 C. applesauce, 1 C. dates, cut small, ½ C. walnuts and beat 1 minute. Pour batter into a well-greased 9 x 12 inch pan and bake at 350 degrees for 45 minutes or until a wooden pick inserted in center of cake comes out clean. Cool 10 minutes. Turn out on a cake rack and when cold, frost with cream cheese frosting.

Cream Cheese Frosting

Beat until smooth and fluffy the following:

1 3-oz. pkg. cream cheese, softened
2 T. soft butter
1 t. vanilla
2 C. sifted powdered sugar

Mabel's Date Bait

Pour 1 C. boiling water over:

1 C. dates, cut up
1 t. soda

Let cool. Cream:
½ C. margarine
1 C. sugar

Add 2 eggs and beat well.
Sift together:
1½ C. flour
¼ t. salt
¾ t. soda

Add dry ingredients alternately to the sugar and margarine with:

1 C. crushed, drained pineapple
⅛ C. pineapple juice

Topping: Mix well:
½ C. walnuts, chopped
½ C. sugar
1 pkg. (6-oz.) chocolate chips

Sprinkle over cake batter and bake at 350 degrees for 30 minutes. (Use a 9 x 13 inch pan.)

German Chocolate Cake

(Adjusted for high altitude)

Melt 1 pkg. (bar) Baker's Sweet Chocolate in ½ C. boiling water and cool.

Cream:
1 C. butter
1¾ C. sugar

Beat until fluffy. Add:
4 egg yolks, unbeaten

one at a time, beating well after each addition. Add chocolate mixture and 1 t. vanilla.

Sift together:
2½ C. plus 1 T. flour, sifted
½ t. salt
¾ t. soda

Add dry ingredients alternately to the chocolate mixture with:

1 C. buttermilk

Beat smooth after each addition. Beat 4 egg whites until stiff and fold, gently, into the batter.

Pour into 3 ungreased, waxpaper-lined layer cake pans, 8 inches in size.

Bake 30 to 40 minutes at 360 degrees F. Cool and frost layers with:

Coconut-Pecan Frosting

Combine:

1 C. evaporated milk
1 C. sugar
3 egg yolks
¼ lb. margarine
1 t. vanilla

Cook over medium heat, stirring constantly until thick, about 12 minutes. Add 1½ C. coconut, 1 C. chopped pecans. Beat until cool and thick.

Alene's Pound Cake

(This is a firm cake and very tasty. I use it for molds such as an Easter Bunny or Santa Claus.)

Cream:
½ C. margarine or butter, softened
1 2/3 C. sugar

Add:
6 medium eggs, one at a time and beating well after each addition

Add:
½ t. lemon or vanilla extract
2 C. flour

Stir well and bake in 3 small greased and floured loaf pans or fancy aluminum molds at 325 degrees for 50 to 60 minutes.

For variation: Add ¼ C. currants.

Never Fail Sour Cream Cake

Beat well 2 eggs

Gradually beat in 1 C. sugar

Add:
1 C. thick sour cream

Mixed with:
¼ t. soda
Sift together and fold in:
1½ C. cake flour, sifted
1 t. baking powder
¼ t. salt

Add:
1 t. vanilla

Pour into greased and floured loaf pan. Bake at 350 degrees for 35 to 40 minutes

Isabel's Crumb Cake

Blend together and reserve 1 C. of mixture for topping:

1¾ C. brown sugar
1 C. flour
½ C. soft shortening

To the remainder add:
1 beaten egg
½ t. salt

Sift together and add:
1 C. flour
½ t. nutmeg
1 t. cinnamon
1 t. soda

Add alternately to the sugar and shortening with:
1 C. buttermilk

Fold in:
½ C. dates, cut
½ C. pecans, chopped

Pour into greased and floured 10 x 10 inch baking pan. Sprinkle with the reserved topping. Bake at 350 degrees for 25 to 30 minutes.

Mom's Red Devil's Food

Dissolve:
2 squares chocolate

in:
1 C. boiling water and reserve

Cream well:
1¾ C. sugar
½ C. butter

Add:
2 egg yolks and beat well

To the sugar, butter, and yolks add:
½ C. sour milk

Alternately with:
2½ C. sifted cake flour
¼ t. salt
¾ t. soda
All sifted together.

Add chocolate mixture and the remaining egg whites, beaten stiff (folding whites in gently!). Bake at 350 degrees for 40 to 45 minutes in a 9 x 12 inch pan, greased and floured.

Yule Cake

This is not only the best fruit cake recipe I know, but it is unique in that all the fruit and nuts are whole, so when cut in slices they resemble a stained glass window!

1½ C. whole Brazil nuts
(To shell Brazil nuts, freeze overnite and crack with hammer. Shell shatters, leaving nut all in one piece. Keep nuts frozen by cracking only a few at a time.
1½ C. walnut halves
1 7-oz. pkg. pitted dates, whole
2/3 C. diced candied orange peel
½ C. red maraschino cherries, whole
½ C. green maraschino cherries, whole
½ C. seedless raisins
1 small pkg. (4-oz.) diced, candied citron
½ C. diced, candied pineapple

Place all the fruit and nuts in a large bowl and pour the following batter over all:

Sift:
¾ C. flour, sifted

with:
¾ C. sugar
½ t. salt
½ t. baking powder

Add:
3 eggs, beaten
1 t. vanilla

Mix well. (There is very little batter, but don't let it worry you!)

Bake in a large bread tin which has been lined with a double layer of greased brown wrapping paper, cut to fit the tin. Bake at 300 degrees F. for about 2 hours or until a wooden pick thrust into center comes out clean. Turn out on a cake rack and remove paper, immediately. Cool. Wrap in foil. (These may be frozen and kept almost indefinitely.)

Mom's Best Gingerbread

Beat all together:
1 C. brown sugar
¾ C. melted shortening
2 eggs
¾ C. molasses

Sift together:
3 C. flour, sifted
1 t. baking powder
½ t. soda
1 t. cinnamon
1 t. ginger
½ t. salt
¼ t. allspice

Add the above alternately to the sugar, shortening and eggs with:

1 C. buttermilk

Bake in a large 9 x 12 inch cake pan at 350 degrees F. for 30 to 35 minutes. Serve with warm Lemon Sauce or whipped cream. (Better yet, with *both*!)

Texas Fruit Cake

Mix well the following ingredients:

1 C. sugar
1 C. flour
2 t. baking powder
½ t. salt

Stir in:
4 well-beaten eggs
1 t. vanilla

Add:
2 lbs. dates (4 cups) cut up
1½ lbs. pecans (6 cups) cut up

Mix well. Divide into three layer cake pans which have been greased and floured, pressing dough well down into pans. Bake at 350 degrees for 5 minutes. Reduce oven temperature to 300 degrees F. and bake 25 minutes more. Ice with carmel icing.

Carmel Icing

First mixture:
Bring to a boil:
2 C. sugar
1 C. milk

Second mixture:
Carmelize 1 C. sugar (place sugar in a heavy pan over medium heat, stir constantly and sugar will begin to brown. When the sugar begins to become light brown, turn heat down and stir rapidly until it is dark brown but be careful not to scorch!) Add the carmelized sugar to the first mixture, along with 1 C. butter. Cook to soft ball stage. Cool and spread on cakes. Mmmmmmmmmmmmmm!

Mayonnaise Fudge Cake

This is a fudge-like, moist cake and best served uniced with soft vanilla ice cream—one of our guest's favorites!

Combine in order given and beat well:

1 C. sugar
1 C. mayonnaise
½ C. cocoa
¼ t. salt
2 C. flour
1½ t. soda
1 C. water
1 t. vanilla

Bake in a 9 x 12 inch baking dish which has been greased and floured, at 350 degrees F. for 25 to 30 minutes or until wooden pick comes out clean when inserted in center of cake.

Oatmeal Cake

This recipe is for those who love a rich, "out-of-this-world" flavor and aroma!

Cover:
1 C. quick-cooking oats

with:
1¼ C. boiling water

and allow to stand until cool, about 20 minutes.

Cream:
½ C. margarine

and:
1 C. brown sugar
1 C. white sugar
2 eggs, beaten

Sift together:
1 1/3 C. flour
1 t. cinnamon
½ t. nutmeg
½ t. salt
1½ t. baking powder

Combine in order given. Bake at 350 degrees F. in a greased and floured 9 x 12 inch pan for about 40 minutes. Frost, when cool, with:

Topping

½ C. butter
1 C. pecans, chopped
½ C. sugar
½ t. vanilla
1 C. coconut
¼ C. canned, condensed milk

Mix ingredients thoroughly and spread on cooled cake. Place under broiler and watch constantly until coconut becomes faintly brown and topping glazes.

Inexpensive "Butter" Sponge Cake

This is an excellent cake for fruit shortcake or making tiny frosted cakes, by cutting in desired shapes, when cool.

Beat very light:
2 eggs

Gradually add:
1 C. sugar (less 2 T. for above 5000 feet)
¼ t. salt

Heat ½ C. milk to boiling point (watch it) with 1 T. butter

Sift:
1 C. sifted flour and
1 t. baking powder

Add the hot milk to the sugar, eggs and salt, and quickly stir in the flour mixture. Have ready a greased and floured 8 x 10 inch pan and rapidly pour batter into it. Bake immediately at 350 degrees for 20 to 25 minutes.

Creole Chocolate Cake

Combine:
1 C. sour cream
1½ C. sugar
¼ C. milk
2 eggs

Sift together and stir into the above:
2 C. flour
¼ t. salt
1 t. baking soda

Melt 3 squares of chocolate in ½ C. hot water, stirring to blend well.

Add to the sour cream the flour mixture.

Bake at 350 degrees for 40 minutes or until a straw comes out clean. When cool, frost with:

1 8-oz. pkg. cream cheese combined with 1 square chocolate, melted in ⅛ C. milk, ¾ to 1 C. sifted powdered sugar. Spread on cake and top with pecan halves.

Yield: 1 9 x 15 inch cake

CANDY & CONFECTIONS

Candied Citrus Peel

This tangy treat will delight you. It is a very good keeper and may be used as a gift item any time of year when one can get thick, perfect peel.

Cut through rind, only, on 3 oranges and 1 or 2 grapefruit (depending on size) and gently peel off skins. Scrape out any membrane that might cling. Cut peels in ¼ inch strips. Place in a large pan, cover with water and bring to a boil, simmer 15 minutes. Drain. Repeat this process two more times, as this removes the bitter taste. Return rind to pan and to it add:

2 C. sugar
1 T. white corn syrup
1 t. ginger
⅛ t. salt
1 C. water

Cook all together, slowly, about 40 minutes, stirring frequently (especially as the syrup becomes absorbed by the peel). When the syrup is nearly absorbed, stir in:

1 t. unflavored gelatin (this is the real secret!)

which has been softened in ½ C. water. When it is cool enough to handle, lift out the rinds, one at a time, and roll in granulated sugar. Lay in a single layer on a cookie sheet and allow to dry for several hours. Store in a tightly covered container.

Cranberry Dainties

In a saucepan, mix 1 1-lb. can jellied cranberry sauce and 1 C. sugar. Beat with electric mixer until nearly smooth. Place over moderate heat and bring to a boil. Remove from heat. Add 1 6-oz. package orange gelatin and stir until dissolved. Add ½ C. walnuts, chopped. Pour into an oiled 9 x 5 inch loaf pan. Chill until firm. Turn out and cut in 1-inch squares. Roll in granulated sugar. Allow to dry in refrigerator, uncovered, 24 hours. Roll again in granulated sugar. Makes 30 squares. (Store, covered, in refrigerator.)

Invest in a candy thermometer! It will pay dividends in results. Use it whenever a thermometer is indicated. Half the fun of making candy is in having perfect results every time!

Date Roll

Combine 2 C. sugar and 1 C. condensed milk. Cook to soft ball stage (235 degrees). Add 1 C. dates, chopped. Cook together until hard ball stage (246 degrees) is reached. Remove from heat and stir in 1 t. vanilla and 1 C. pecans or walnuts, chopped. Cool to lukewarm. Beat until thickened and turn out on a board and knead until it holds its shape. Shape in a roll and wrap in a damp cloth until cold. When ready to serve, slice as desired.

Never Fail Fudge (An Old Standby)

Boil over medium heat for 10 minutes:
4½ C. sugar
1 can (13-oz.) evaporated milk

Stir constantly. Turn off heat and add:
1 pt. marshmallow cream
2 pkg. chocolate chips
2 regular size Hershey bars
½ C. butter

Stir until well blended. Add 2 C. walnuts or pecans, chopped. (Optional) Pour into a buttered pan. Cool. Cut in squares.

Doesn't anyone pull taffy anymore? Maybe this isn't what the kids do on Halloween night these days, but it was part of the fun—once, long ago—maybe it's gone along with pushin' over the Chic Sales and stickin' a pin in the button on the doorbell. Here's a real good recipe which might bring back memories for you!

Vinegar Taffy

Combine and bring to a boil:
4 C. sugar
1½ C. water
½ C. vinegar

Boil the the hard ball (cracking—240 degrees) stage. Add 1 t. vanilla. Turn out on a well-buttered platter. When cool enough to handle, divide in two and with well-buttered hands, pull until it changes color and stays firm enough to hold shape when replaced on platter. Crack into pieces. Eat along with fresh, ripe apples! Those were the days! (The above recipe should be pulled by four people—two on each half!)

Best-Ever Peanut Brittle

Cook to soft ball stage (235 degrees):
1½ C. sugar
1½ C. white syrup
½ C. water

Add:
1 lb. (2 C.) *raw* peanuts
1½ T. butter
¼ t. salt

Cook slowly until the mixture makes *threads* of the syrup when the spoon is raised above the pan. Watch carefully, stirring constantly until the syrup looks as if it might burn and the peanuts are flecked with brown. Remove from heat. Add 1½ t. vanilla and 3 level teaspoons of soda. Beat vigorously as it foams. Pour onto a buttered cookie sheet. When cool, crack in pieces, and store in tightly covered containers; it will keep several weeks.

Luscious Glazed Almonds

This is a wonderful gift item or just for nibbling! So easy, too!

In a heavy skillet combine:
1 C. whole blanched almonds
½ C. sugar
2 T. butter

Heat over medium heat, stir constantly, until almonds are toasted and covered with the sugar, which should be golden brown—about 15 minutes. Stir in:

½ t. vanilla

Spread on foil to cool and sprinkle lightly with salt. Cool and break into small clusters.

Holiday Walnuts

Toast 2½ C. walnuts in a moderate oven (350 degrees) for 10 to 12 minutes, stirring once or twice.

Butter the sides of a 2-qt. saucepan and in it combine:

1½ C. sugar
½ C. water
¼ C. honey
½ t. cinnamon
½ t. salt

Bring to a boil, stirring constantly to dissolve the sugar. Cook to soft ball state (235 degrees) without stirring. Remove from heat and beat until it only *starts* to become creamy (this sets up very fast). Add 1 t. vanilla and the toasted walnuts. Stir carefully until nuts are coated and mixture thickens. Turn out on a buttered cookie sheet and separate nuts, at once.

CASSEROLE DISHES

Many men look upon this so-called "one-dish-meal" with disfavor. I believe it's mainly because it often looks thrown together—as my daughter laughingly comments, "something from the back of the refrigerator, with cheese sauce."

When one concocts our Magic potion, let's try to put it together with a bit of eye appeal, taking care nothing *looks* left-over. A left-over can really be the basis for a real gourmet meal. Put a bit of color into a drab-looking dish by adding a bit of parsley or pimento, or both. Layer your foods rather than tossing all together—use your imagination! Don't let a long list of ingredients scare you or make it seem it's too difficult—remember a casserole is almost completely a meal which can be prepared in advance—leaving the cook free at mealtime! A wonderful idea!

Peg's Slumgulion

Cook 4 slices of bacon, diced, in a large frying pan. Remove bacon, crumble and reserve. To the 2 T. bacon fat, in the pan,

Add:
1 lb. lean pork, cubed
1 lb. beef chuck, cubed

Sprinkle with 1½ t. salt and brown lightly.

Add:
1 small onion, diced
2 T. green pepper, diced
1 C. cream style corn
1 can cream of mushroom soup
1 C. fresh frozen peas, cooked
½ C. cheddar cheese, diced
1 7-oz. pkg. noodles, cooked, drained

Stir gently and place all ingredients, including the crumbled bacon, in a large casserole (2-qt.). Top with a few buttered crumbs and a bit of grated cheddar cheese. Bake at 325 degrees for 2 hours or until meat is tender. Serves 6 generously.

This is a good "keeper" in case of latecomers!

Cheeseburger Pie

Having company and running out of ideas for lunch—here's one that will bring you lots of compliments—different, too!

Crumble together with a pastry blender or your fingertips:

1 C. sifted flour
½ t. salt
1/3 C. soft shortening

Gradually add, and mix in with a fork:
2½ T. water

Form into a round ball and on a lightly floured board, roll in a 10-inch circle to fit a 9-inch pie place, and allowing 1 inch extra dough to turn under at edge for fluting.

Brown:
1 lb. ground chuck in
2 T. fat

Add:
1 t. salt
⅛ t. pepper
½ t. oregano
1 small onion, diced
2 T. green pepper, minced

Cook until vegetables are tender but not browned.

Add:
½ C. dry bread crumbs
½ can (8-oz.) tomato sauce with mushrooms

Mix well and turn into the unbaked pastry shell. Top with cheese topping:

Beat well 1 egg and add:
1 C. sharp cheddar cheese, grated
¼ C. milk
½ t. salt
½ t. dry mustard
½ t. worchestershire sauce

Pour the mixture over the meat, filling in the crust. Bake in a hot oven 425 degrees for 20 minutes. Reduce heat to 325 degrees and bake 15 minutes more. Serve in wedges with sauce made of the remaining ½ can tomato sauce and 3 T. chili sauce, heated to boiling point.

Casserole Rex

In a large fry pay, slowly brown:
6 center-cut pork chops, thick cut (¾-inch)

Remove chops from pan and reserve. In the pan, saute:
1 C. diced celery
1 small onion, chopped
1 clove garlic, crushed

When vegetables are tender but not brown, add:
1 can tomato soup
1 C. water
1 t. oregano
1 small bay leaf
½ t. dry mustard
1 16-oz. can okra, drained
1 can whole kernel corn with juice
1 C. raw rice, regular

Combine well and turn into a 2-qt. casserole. Top with pork chops. Cover. Bake at 350 degrees for 1 hour or until rice is tender.

Corn Creole

In 2 T. shortening, saute:
1 lb. ground beef.

When brown, add:
1 small onion, minced
1 clove garlic, crushed
1 small green pepper, diced

Cook until vegetables are tender but not brown. Add:
1 t. chile powder
1½ t. salt
1½ C. canned tomatoes
1 C. cream style corn
½ C. yellow corn meal

Bring slowly to a boil, stirring constantly. Add:
1 C. milk
1/3 C. chopped ripe olives

Pour into a well-greased 1½-qt. casserole. Bake at 325 degrees for one hour.

Bee's Baked Chop Suey

Brown: 1 lb. hamburger
in: 2 T. fat

Add:
1 C. celery, sliced thin
½ C. onion, diced
1 small green pepper, diced

Cook vegetables until tender—not brown.

Add:
2 T. soy sauce
1 can cream of mushroom soup
1 can cream of chicken soup

Stir gently and heat to boiling point. Turn off heat. In the meantime, cook 1½ C. Minute Rice according to the directions on the package. In a greased baking dish (10 x 10 inches), place the cooked rice, and cover with the meat sauce. Bake at 350 degrees for ¾ hour. Sprinkle the contents of 1 3-oz. can Chow Mein Noodles over the top and bake an additional 15 minutes. Serves 6.

Cabbage Rolls, De Luxe

Remove 12 leaves from a large head of cabbage (pare off thick center a bit) and pour boiling water over them to make them pliable. Drain well. Pat with a paper towel to dry.

Combine:
2 C. ground cooked ham
and
2 C. cooked, fine noodles

Mix gently:
½ C. seedless raisins
1 egg, beaten
1 T. mustard (salad style)

Divide the mixture between the 12 cabbage leaves. Fold the leaves around the filling and secure with toothpicks. Place rolls in a greased baking dish 9 x 13 inches and cover with the following sauce:

2 8-oz. cans tomato sauce with cheese
1 7¾-oz. jar junior chopped carrots
1 T. brown sugar
½ C. water
¼ t. allspice
¼ t. salt

Cover with foil and bake at 350 degrees for 35 minutes. Remove cover and bake 10 minutes longer.

Baked Tuna Stuffed Avocado

In a bowl combine:
1 7-oz. can tuna, drained and flaked
¼ t. salt
¾ C. finely chopped celery
2 T. grated onion
¼ C. mayonnaise
¼ t. curry powder

Halve 3 avocados, unpeeled. Remove the seeds and fill the cavity with the above mixture, dividing it equally among the six halves. Place in a shallow baking dish and carefully pour enough boiling water into the dish to cover the bottom. Sprinkle the tops of each half with a bit of Parmesan cheese. Bake at 375 degrees for 20 minutes, or until well heated. Crush 1/3 C. potato chips and sprinkle over the avocados. Return to oven for 3 minutes. Serves 6.

(Served with a salad of fresh, ripe tomatoes, sliced, and cucumber slices—it is a mighty tasty luncheon. You may want to add a muffin—it will be all you need—and quick, too!)

Leone's Mystery Casserole

Cook:
1 6-oz. pkg. noodles as directed on pkg.

In 2 T. butter, saute:
1 onion, chopped
1 clove garlic, crushed

When tender, add:
1 can cream style corn
2 3-oz. cans mushroom pieces
1 med. can tamales, cut in 1-inch pieces
1 flat can tuna
1 T. worchestershire sauce
1 t. salt
¼ t. pepper
½ t. chili powder

Combine all ingredients, gently, and bake in a 2-qt. casserole at 350 degrees for 45 minutes.

Mazumi

In a large frying pan, slowly brown:
2 lbs. fresh lean pork, ground

Add:
2 large onions, chopped

Cook until onions are tender. Add:
2½ C. canned tomatoes
2 t. salt
¼ t. pepper
1 T. brown sugar

Mix well. Remove from heat and add:
1 12-pz. pkg. wide noodles, cooked
1 C. grated cheddar cheese

Turn into a 2-qt. casserole and top with an additional:
1 C. grated cheddar cheese.

Bake at 350 degrees for one hour. Serves 8.

(This is a large recipe and you might like to divide the mixture between two smaller casseroles and freeze one for future use. Cut down the baking time to 50 minutes, or until well browned. It is not necessary to bake the one you freeze—bake it later!)

Cauliflower-Crab Meat Au Gratin

This recipe title is a perfectly delicious dish for those of you who like cauliflower—it all tastes like crab meat, really!

1 large head of cauliflower, sliced

(You should have about 4 C.) Parboil the slices in 2 C. rapidly boiling water for 3 minutes. Drain well!

Combine:
1½ C. milk
3 T. *instant* flour

in a saucepan. Bring slowly to a boil and cook 3 minutes, stirring constantly.

Add:
the precooked cauliflower
2 T. butter
1 t. salt
¾ C. sharp cheddar cheese, grated
½ t. oregano

Stir gently. In a 1-qt. casserole, alternate the above mixture with:

2 6-oz. cans crab meat, flaked

ending with the first mixture. Top with ½ C. soft bread crumbs which have been tossed with 3 T. melted butter. Bake at 350 degrees for 40 minutes or until crumbs are nicely browned.

Corned Beef Casserole

(for Economy Plus!)

1 6-oz. pkg. elbow macaroni, cooked
1 12-oz. can corned beef, cubed
¼ lb. (½ C.) cheddar cheese, cubed
1 can cream of mushroom soup
¾ C. milk
1 small onion, diced

Combine all ingredients, stirring gently. Turn into a 1-qt. casserole and top with ¾ C. dry bread crumbs which have been mixed with 2 T. melted butter. Bake at 350 degrees for 45 minutes.

Swirl-Top Casserole

Melt:
4 T. butter in a saucepan

Add:
4 T. flour, stirring constantly

Add:
2 C. milk

Cook over medium heat, stirring until smooth and thickened.

Add:
2 hard-cooked eggs, sliced
2 6-oz. cans boned chicken
½ C. green, stuffed olives, sliced
½ t. dried, minced onion
¼ t. celery salt
½ t. salt
⅛ t. pepper

Prepare 2 C. prepared biscuit mix as directed on the package, pat gently into a rectangle (about 9 x 6 inches). Sprinkle with ¾ C. grated cheddar cheese and roll up, jelly-roll fashion. Slice into ½-inch slices and place in overlapping circle around edge of casserole. (Filling in casserole should be piping hot when biscuits are added.) Bake 15 to 20 minutes at 425 degrees or until biscuits have raised and are well browned. During last 5 minutes of baking, cover each swirl with a thin slice of jellied cranberry sauce.

Saucy Stuffed Romaine

Combine:
1 lb. ground beef or lamb
1 C. rice, cooked
1 small onion, minced
1 t. caraway seed
1 t. salt
¼ t. pepper
1 egg, unbeaten

Pour boiling water over 12 large leaves of romaine (if leaves are not large enough, use two, overlapping to contain the filling). Allow to stand 5 minutes. Drain well. Divide the mixture between the 12 leaves and roll up securely with cord, as a package. Brown in 3 T. fat. Place in a shallow baking dish (13 x 9 inches) and cover with sauce.

Sauce: In a saucepan combine:
1¼ C. tomatoes
¼ C. raisins
3 T. lemon juice
1 T. brown sugar
¼ t. salt
¼ C. crumbled gingersnaps

Simmer sauce slowly ½ hour and pour over Romaine Rolls. Bake at 350 degrees for 45 minutes.

(There are many casserole dishes included in this cookbook under other categories. See cheese, rice, vegetable, fish, meat, and also foreign recipe chapters.)

CHEESE & EGG DISHES

Swiss Asparagus Pie

This is a variation of Quiche Lorraine—but for those who like asparagus (and who doesn't!), it is superb! Surprise your guests or family at luncheon by serving a wedge of this pie, with a "Blushing Pear" Salad, a hot roll, and Lemon Dainty!

Combine:
1¼ C. flour
¾ t. salt
½ C. soft shortening

Stir in with a fork:
3 or 4 T. cold water, adding

a bit at a time, until mixture holds together. Roll out on a lightly floured board to fit a deep 9-inch pie plate. Flute rim and prick well with a fork. Bake at 425 degrees for 10 minutes. Remove from oven and lower heat to 350 degrees.

In the meantime, cook 1 lb. of fresh asparagus. Drain and reserve.

Scald:
1½ C. milk with
2 T. butter
½ t. salt
½ t. worchestershire sauce

Beat 3 eggs slightly in medium size bowl. *Gradually* add the scalded milk mixture to eggs, mixing well. Grate 1 C. natural Swiss cheese. Arrange half the asparagus in prebaked shell; cover with half the grated cheese. Repeat with remaining asparagus and cheese. Pour the milk mixture over all carefully. Sprinkle lightly with a bit of paprika. Bake at 350 degrees for 30 minutes. (Do not overbake, as this filling will set after it stands.) Cool 5 minutes. Cut into 6 wedges. Serves 6.

Margaret Reedy's Fondue

In the cooking dish of a fondue set, crush 1 clove of garlic with ½ t. salt (or put garlic through a press). Place boiling water in lower section of fondue set and light the fuel, setting opening for medium heat. Add to the cooker 2 C. Sauterne wine (this may be warmed on the stove to hasten cooking procedure). Grate 4 C. natural Swiss cheese (aged, preferred). Toss the cheese with:

3 T. flour
⅛ t. pepper
¼ t. nutmeg
2 T. Kirsch

Gradually add the cheese to the hot wine in the cooking pan; it will become thick and a bit "stringy." Serve at the table and pass cubes of French bread and dark sweet rye bread.

To eat: Stab cube with a fork and roll quickly in the fondue. Pop the luscious morsel in your mouth before it falls off your fork! It's a fun thing—and delicious. Served with a tossed salad and a tiny glass of Kirsch, it's an unbeatable "Saturday Night"! A simple fruit dessert would be appropriate. Serves 4.

Bee's Eggs Exotica

Cook 8 eggs to hard-boiled stage. Shell and cut in half, lengthwise. Remove yolks to a bowl and mash smooth. To the yolks add:

1/3 C. mayonnaise
½ t. *each* salt, curry powder, paprika
¼ t. dry mustard.

Refill egg whites with the above mixture.

In a saucepan blend:
4 T. melted butter
2 T. flour

Stir in:
1 can frozen shrimp soup, undiluted
1 soup can of water

Add:
½ C. grated cheddar cheese

Cook 5 minutes at low heat. Arrange the egg halves in a shallow baking dish (10 x 6 inches) and cover with the sauce. Combine 1 C. soft bread crumbs and 3 T. melted butter and sprinkle over top. Bake at 350 degrees for 20 minutes or until well heated and crumbs are lightly brown. Trim with parsley. Serves 6.

Egg Curry

Cook 10 eggs to hard-boiled stage. Shell and cut in half, lengthwise

Combine:
1 can cream of mushroom soup
½ C. milk
2 t. curry powder
½ small onion, grated

Simmer gently about 5 minutes.

Cook 2 C. Minute Rice as directed on the package. Arrange the rice in center of a warmed platter with the egg halves around the outside. Spoon sauce over the eggs and rice. In small, separate bowls arrange the condiments which may be added to individual taste: dry-roasted, salted peanuts, white or dark raisins, mandarin oranges, drained, and flaked coconut—any or all may be used. Suit yourself!

Sophie's Eggs Bombay

Saute, in 3 T. butter, 2 C. chopped onion until tender but not browned.

Add:
1 C. sour cream
1 t. curry powder
½ t. salt
⅛ t. pepper

Turn into a shallow baking dish (10 x 6 inches). On the top of the sauce, make 4 or 5 indentations and break an egg into each (4 or 5 eggs). Grate ¾ C. cheddar cheese over all and dust lightly with paprika. Bake at 325 degrees about 25 minutes or until eggs are set.

Sunday Mornin' Eggs

In a medium bowl combine:

6 eggs
½ t. salt
⅛ t. pepper
¼ C. milk
½ t. rosemary

In a skillet, melt 3 T. butter over medium heat. Turn in egg mixture as it cooks; gently lift eggs from bottom and fold over to cook lightly. Just before eggs reach the degree of doneness you like, fold in ½ C. creamed cottage cheese, well drained. Heat through and serve 4!

Cheese and Sausage Baked Potatoes

Bake 4 medium size baking potatoes at 400 degrees for one hour or until tender. When tender, cut a lengthwise slice from the top of each potato. Scoup out the insides, being careful not to break the shell. Mash well with:

2 or 3 T. milk
1 T. butter
1 egg yolk
1 t. salt
⅛ t. pepper
1/3 C. diced, processed smoky cheese

Refill the shells with the above mixture.

In the meantime, slowly cook 8 Brown and Serve sausages. Tuck 2 sausages into the tops of each of the 4 potatoes and return to the oven (400 degrees) and bake an additional 15 minutes or until well heated. Serves 4.

The reason I have said "gently" so many times in the egg cooking recipes is that "easy does it." High heat ruins egg dishes, and we want to come up with a tender product. The only exception is in cooking an omelet—even then care is needed.

Spanish Omelet

Sauce:
Saute 1 small onion, minced.
1 clove garlic, crushed

in:
2 T. butter

Add:
2 T. chopped ripe olives
1 3½-oz. can mushroom pieces
1 8-oz. can tomato sauce
1 T. parsley, minced
¼ t. salt
⅛ t. pepper
¼ t. oregano

Cook gently, uncovered, for 10 minutes, until sauce becomes thickened. Keep warm. In a medium size bowl, combine:

6 eggs
10 T. water
½ t. salt
¼ t. pepper

Beat with a fork only until whites of eggs are well mixed with the yolks. Heat skillet (preferably Teflon) and add 3 T. butter. When butter begins to sizzle, add egg mixture. With a spatula, lift the mixture gently, allowing the uncooked portion to run underneath. As it cooks, fold all at one time to the opposite side of pan. Gently turn back and remove from heat. Serve on a warm platter with Spanish sauce on top. Decorate with parsley. Serves 4.

Egg and Asparagus Casserole

8 hard-cooked eggs, shelled and sliced
2 C. fresh asparagus, cut and cooked 5 minutes

In a saucepan combine:
1½ C. milk
3 T. instant flour
¾ t. salt
dash pepper

Cook over medium heat, stirring constantly until thickened. Add 1, 4-oz. can mushroom pieces, drained. Combine sauce with eggs and asparagus and turn into a buttered baking dish (1½-qt. size). Bake at 350 degrees for 20 minutes. Serve on English muffins, toasted, or toast points.

Denver Scramble

Heat 2 T. butter in a skillet and stir in:

½ C. onion, minced
½ C. green pepper, minced
½ C. cooked ham, chopped

Cook together, gently, until vegetables are tender but not brown.

In a bowl, combine 6 eggs, 6 T. water, ½ t. salt, and a dash of tabasco sauce. Beat only until well mixed. Add the eggs to the mixture in the skillet and stir gently until eggs are set. Serve with hot buttermilk biscuits. Serves 4.

Quick Eggs, Florentine

Cook 2 pkgs. fresh frozen leaf spinach, according to directions on the package. Drain and chop well (slicing on a board with a sharp knife does the job fine). Line a shallow baking dish (10 x 6 inches) with the spinach. Break 6 eggs in hollows made in the spinach "nest." Heat togethr 1 can cream of celery soup and 1 C. grated cheese. Pour this sauce around the eggs on the spinach. Cover with an additional ½ C. grated cheese and bake at 350 degrees for 25 minutes or until eggs are set. Very nice dinner dish!

Serve with sliced fresh tomatoes and a salad made of grapefruit and avocado with Russian dressing!

Eggs in Sour Cream Sauce

In a skillet, cook:
¾ C. green onions and tops, chopped

in:
2 T. butter until onions are tender,

over medium heat. Lower heat under pan and break 6 eggs onto the onions (do not break yolks). Cover.

Mix:
1 C. sour cream
1 T. sweet pickle relish
½ t. salt
⅛ t. pepper

and pour over eggs. Cover. Simmer gently until eggs are set—about 10 minutes. Serves 3 (2 eggs each).

COOKIES

There is no end to the number of fine cookie recipes today. Everyone has his own favorites, and these are only a few of mine—some are old, some are new.

Nestle's Magic Cookie Bar

This is a recipe I want you to have at hand because it's easy and delicious—developed by Nestle's.

In a baking pan 13 inches by 9 inches, melt ½ C. butter or margarine. When melted, sprinkle with 1½ C. graham cracker crumbs. Over the crumbs sprinkle 1 C. walnuts, chopped. Sprinkle nuts with 1 C. Nestle's chocolate chips. Over the chocolate chips spread 1 1/3 C. flaked coconut. Over all, evenly pour: 1 1/3 C. (15-oz. can) Eagle Brand Sweetened Condensed Milk. (Do not stir!) Bake at 350 degrees 25 minutes or until top of it is lightly browned. Cool in pan 15 minutes. Cut in bars. Makes about 2 dozen bars.

Mama's Chocolate Chip Coconut Cookies

Cream:
½ C. shortening
¼ C. brown sugar
½ C. white sugar

Add:
1 egg, beaten

1 C. flour
Sifted with:
½ t. salt
½ t. soda

Add:
1 t. vanilla
1 pkg. (8-oz.) chocolate chips
1 pkg. (7-oz.) coconut

Mix well. Drop by teaspoonfuls onto a greased baking sheet. Bake at 350 degrees for 10 to 12 minutes, until *lightly* browned. Makes about 4 dozen cookies.

Renie's Chinese Chews

Sift together:
¾ C. flour
¼ t. salt
1 t. baking powder
1 C. sugar

Stir in:
3 eggs, beaten
1 C. dates, chopped
1 C. walnuts, chopped

Bake in a greased pan (10 inches by 14 inches) at 300 degrees for 30 minutes. Cool. Cut into bars and roll in sifted powdered sugar. Makes about 2 dozen cookies.

Molasses Crinkles

(Delicious and so professional looking!)

Cream:
¾ C. shortening
1 C. brown sugar

Add:
1 egg, beaten
4 T. molasses

Sift together;
2¼ C. flour
¼ t. salt
2 t. soda
½ t. cloves
1 t. cinnamon
1 t. ginger

Mix all together until well blended. Make into balls about the size of a walnut. Dip one side in granulated sugar and place sugar-side up on a lightly greased cookie sheet about 2 inches apart. Sprinkle each cookie with a drop of two of water. (This glazes the top.) Bake at 350 degrees, 12 to 15 minutes or until firm. Makes about 5 dozen cookies.

Fruit Cake Cookies

(Good any time of year!)

Cream:
½ C. butter or margarine
1 C. sugar

Add:
2 eggs, unbeaten
3 T. water

Sift together:
1½ C. flour, sifted
½ t. salt
½ t. cinnamon
½ t. soda

Mix with the creamed mixture until well blended.

Add:
2 C. dates, cut in small pieces
1 C. mixed candied fruit
1 C. walnuts, chopped
2 C. filberts, chopped (optional)

Mix well. Drop by teaspoonfuls onto a greased cookie sheet, 2 inches apart, and bake at 350 degrees for 12 to 15 minutes or until firm and delicately brown. Store in a tightly covered container—a good keeper, if you can! Makes about 5 dozen cookies.

Rosettes

This recipe requires rosette irons in fancy patterns, but it's well worth the small cost, in beauty! The irons must be heated in hot salad oil, such as Mazola, and dipped into the cookie batter. Best results come from using an electric skillet to insure even temperature in cooking.

Method: In an electric skillet put enough best quality salad oil to reach a depth of about 1¼ inches. Set control at 380 degrees in Colorado (350 degrees at lower altitudes). Rest the rosette irons in the fat. When the light goes out on the control, both the fat and the irons are at the proper temperature.

Cookie batter:

Combine and beat well:

2 eggs, beaten slightly
1 T. sugar
¼ t. salt
1 C. flour, sifted
1 C. milk (less 1 T. milk)
1 t. vanilla

Drain excess fat from rosette iron and dip iron, *only to the top* (not over) into the batter. Batter will adhere to the iron. Immediately immerse the iron, with batter, into the hot fat. The cookie will fall off in a moment, into the fat. Turn quickly, once or twice—do *not* brown—remove to paper towels to drain. (A pair of tongs is a wonderful help here!) Repeat process until all batter is used. Practice will make perfect cookies! When cold, dust with sifted powdered sugar. Makes about 4 dozen.

Spritz Cookies

Here, too, a small investment in a Spritz Cookie machine (similar to cake decorator) pays dividends of beauty! These are a delightful holiday cookie—decorate as fancy as you like with colored sugars, bits of cherries and citron—or let your imagination run rampant. Follow the directions that you will receive with your machine. Here is a fine recipe.

Cream:
1 C. butter (no substitute, please)
1 C. sugar

Add:
2 eggs and beat well
1 t. almond extract
2½ C. flour

Combine until well blended. Put dough into cookie press, using various shapes. Bake at 350 degrees about 5 minutes. Watch carefully, as they should be only delicately colored, not browned. Touch with fingertip to check firmness. Makes approximately 5 dozen cookies.

Black Walnut Crescents

Cream:

½ C. butter (no substitutes, please!)

3 T. sugar

1 C. flour

1 C. ground black walnuts

Combine all ingredients. Shape a teaspoonful of dough into a crescent shape. Repeat until all dough is used. Bake at 325 degrees for 20 minutes on ungreased cookie sheets (using top rack in oven, so bottom of cookies do not brown too fast). Cool. Dust with sifted powdered sugar. Makes about 3 dozen cookies.

Double Peanut Bumps

Cream:
1 C. soft shortening
1 C. sugar
1 C. brown sugar
1 C. peanut butter

Add:
2 eggs and mix well
1 t. vanilla

Sift together:
2½ C. flour, sifted
1½ t. soda

Mix all ingredients together until well blended. Add and stir well:

1 C. coarsely chopped peanuts

Shape into balls the size of walnuts and place on an ungreased cookie sheet. Flatten with the bottom of a glass, dipped in granulated sugar. Bake at 350 degrees about 10 minutes. Makes 5 dozen cookies.

Aunt Nora's Springerli

Beat 4 eggs until light and gradually add 1 lb. powdered sugar. Beat 10 minutes.

Add:
¼ t. salt
¼ t. anise oil (or lemon extract)
¼ C. butter, melted

Sift together:
4 C. flour
1 t. baking powder

Mix all together. The dough should be smooth and stiff. (Add a little additional flour if needed.) Place dough in refrigerator to chill. Roll out about a third of the dough at a time (keeping the rest refrigerated) to a thickness of ¼ inch. Flour top very lightly. Flour a springerli rolling pin, lightly, and press on the rolled dough to imprint the pattern. Cut apart on imprinted squares. Place on brown paper. Do not cover. Leave overnight to dry out. Next day, place on *bright* aluminum cookie pans and bake at 275 degrees for about 12 minutes. Do not brown. These keep indefinitely and can be frozen in plastic bags or airtight containers.

Lemon Bars

Mix together until well blended:

1 C. flour
½ C. butter (no substitutes, please!)
¼ C. powdered sugar

Pat into a lightly buttered pan 9 by 9 inches. Bake 20 minutes at 350 degrees.

Combine:
2 eggs
1 C. sugar
3 T. lemon juice
⅛ t. lemon rind, grated

Beat until well blended. Pour over prebaked crust and return to oven (350 degrees); bake 25 minutes longer. Makes about 2 dozen bars. Best eaten fresh!

English Toffee Squares

Cream together:
1 C. butter
1 C. brown sugar

Add:
1 egg yolk
1 t. vanilla
2 C. flour
⅛ t. salt

Combine all ingredients and blend well. Bake in a greased pan 10 by 10 inches at 350 degrees for 20 minutes. While cookies are hot, cover with:

8 oz. sweet chocolate, shaved fine

Cover chocolate with:

½ C. walnuts, chopped

Cool. Cut into squares. Makes about 2 dozen.

Mrs. Julyan's Date-Filled Cookies

Grind 2 cups oats (quick-cooking style). Reserve.

Cream:
1½ C. sugar
1 C. shortening (part butter)

Add:
1 egg
½ C. sour milk
1 t. soda
2 C. flour
½ t. baking powder

Mix well and add:

2 C. *ground* oatmeal (reserved)

Blend well and roll out on a lightly floured board. Cut in rounds. Place a tablespoon of filling on half the rounds. Cover with remaining halves. Press edges to seal. Bake at 350 degrees for 10 to 15 minutes or until lightly browned.

Filling:
Combine in a saucepan:
1 lb. dates, cut fine
¾ C. water
¾ C. sugar
2 t. vanilla

Cook until thick. Cool. Use as before mentioned. A very filling, satisfying cookie!

Yummy Cookies

Combine: 1 C. shortening
With: 1 C. sugar
Add:
2 eggs, well beaten
1 t. vanilla

Sift together and add to the above:

1½ C. flour
½ t. salt
1 t. baking powder.

Blend well and spread batter into a greased pan 10 by 13 inches. Cover with the following topping:

Stiffly beat:
2 egg whites

Gradually beat in:
¼ C. brown sugar
¼ C. white sugar

Fold in 1 C. slivered almonds. Bake at 350 degrees for 30 to 35 minutes. Makes about 2 dozen bars.

Orange-Date Bars

In a saucepan, combine:

½ pound dates, cut up
16 orange jelly slices (candy), sliced thin
½ C. sugar
¾ C. water
2 T. flour

Cook together, stirring constantly until transparent and orange slices have melted. Cool.

While filling cools, cream together:

1 C. shortening (less 2 T. shortening)
¾ C. brown sugar
¼ C. white sugar

Add:
1 t. soda dissolved in 1 t. hot water
3 T. *hot* milk
2 C. flour
¼ t. salt

Blend well and pat one half the dough into a buttered pan (9 by 13 inches). Cover with filling. Roll out the remaining dough on a lightly floured board to the approximate size of the pan. Cut in strips (as dough is rich) and lift with a spatula to place over the date-orange filling. Press down with fingertips. Bake at 350 degrees for about 40 minutes or until top is light brown. Makes about 24 cookies.

Sour Cream Cookies

(An 1889 recipe)

Cream:
1 C. butter

With:
1 C. sugar

Add:
4 egg yolks

Combine:
2/3 C. sour cream and
2 t. soda

Add:
Flour (about 2¼ C.)

Add flour *gradually* to the above—only enough to make the dough possible to handle. (The secret is to use as little flour as possible, keeping dough *soft* but stiff enough to roll lightly.) Roll and cut with a scalloped cookie cutter dipped in flour. Sprinkle with sugar and cinnamon mixture and press a raisin into center of each. Bake on a lightly greased cookie sheet at 325 degrees, 8 to 10 minutes or until firm and lightly colored. Makes about 4 dozen.

DESSERTS

Pick some rainy or snowy day and try your hand at some desserts that will freeze for later use. Some people clean out the dresser drawers on days like this, but you'll have a lot more fun if you get cozy in your kitchen and whip up a few goodies. Here are only a few of the countless recipes for dessert—hope you will like them.

Applesauce Torte

In a large saucepan, melt ¼ C. butter and stir in 2 C. crushed graham cracker crumbs (about 20 crackers). Add ½ t. cinnamon and mix well. In an 8- or 9-inch spring-form pan, pat half the mixture. Reserve the remainder for top.

Filling:
Separate 2 eggs and beat the yolks until light in color. Stir in 1 15-oz. can sweetened condensed Eagle Brand milk and the grated rind and juice of one lemon. Add 2 cups *thick* applesauce.

Beat the remaining 2 egg whites until they hold firm peaks. Fold gently into the above mixture. Pour all into the spring-form pan, over the crumbs. Top with reserved crumb mixture. Bake at 325 degrees for 1 hour or until torte is firm. (Jiggle the pan slightly to check this!) Cool in pan. May be served with a bit of whipped cream, if desired.

This custard tart is mighty fancy looking for the little work involved.

Custard Apple Tart

Crust:
1½ C. sifted flour
½ t. salt
½ C. shortening

Crumble the above with your fingertips until the mixture resembles cornmeal. Gradually add 4 or 5 T. water to bind together. Shape into a ball and roll out on a lightly floured board to a 13-inch circle. Place in a 10-inch spring form pan and flute the edges deeply. Over the crust sprinkle a mixture of:

1/3 C. dry bread crumbs
¼ C. sugar
1 t. cinnamon
¼ t. salt

Pare, core, and slice 6 C. apples and arrange over the crumb mixture in the crust, in a neat swirl pattern. Dot with ¼ C. (½ stick) butter and bake in a hot oven (425 degrees) for 15 minutes. Reduce heat to 350 degrees and cover the apples with mixture of:

3 eggs, beaten thick
1 C. heavy cream
¼ C. sugar
¼ t. nutmeg

Bake at 350 degrees about 30 minutes or until a silver knife inserted in center comes out clean. Remove from oven.

In a small saucepan, over low heat, melt:

½ C. apricot preserves with 2 drops red food coloring

When smooth, spoon this glaze over the hot tart and sprinkle with:

1/3 C. toasted, slivered almonds

When cool, remove sides from spring form and place on your prettiest serving plate. Food for any king! Serves about 10 people.

Leone's Honeycomb Pudding

In a large bowl combine:

½ C. flour
½ C. sugar
½ C. butter

Add:
4 eggs, well beaten

Stir in:
1 C. dark Karo syrup

Add:
1 t. soda
1 t. vanilla

Beat all ingredients well. Turn into the top of a *one-and-one-half-quart* size double boiler. Steam slowly over simmering water for 2 hours. The secret: Don't peek! Serve with a little dollop of soft ice cream.

Serves 8.

This is a very light dessert—nice to use following a hearty meal.

Slush

Mash 3 medium-size bananas with the juice from 2 small lemons (about 1/3 C.).

Add:
1 C. sugar
1 No. 2 can crushed pineapple and juice
2 C. orange juice (fresh or frozen)
2 C. gingerale

Mix well and turn into a large freezer tray. As it freezes, stir once or twice. At serving time, let stand at room temperature and serve in a slushy state in chilled glass dishes.

Serves about 8.

Apple Pie-Cake

Combine:
¼ C. butter
1 C. sugar

Beat in:
1 egg

Sift together and add to the above:
1 C. flour
¼ t. salt
½ t. cinnamon
½ t. nutmeg
1 t. soda stirred into 2 T. hot water

Combine well and mix in:
2½ C. diced raw apples
½ C. nuts, chopped
1 t. vanilla

Turn into a greased 10- by 13-inch baking dish. Bake at 350 degrees for 45 minutes. May be served with whipped cream or soft ice cream, if desired.

About 20 servings.

Pink Fruit Torte

Put through a grinder, *keeping colors separate*:

½ lb. white Nabisco wafers
½ lb. pink Nabisco wafers

Grind:
1 C. apples (2 large apples)
1 C. cranberries
1 C. crushed pineapple, well drained

Add:
1 C. sugar and mix well. Let stand 20 minutes.

In a bowl, beat until light and creamy:
¼ lb. soft butter
1½ C. sifted powdered sugar
1 egg

In a pan (9 by 13 inches), place the white crumbs. Spread the butter and sugar mixture over the crumbs. Cover with the fruit mixture.

Beat 1 C. whipping cream until it holds its shape. Spread over the fruit. Top all with the pink wafer crumbs. Refrigerate 8 hours or overnight.

Makes 12 generous portions.

This is beautiful—it should please the ladies' luncheon!

A delightful, refreshing dessert:

Pineapple With Sour Cream

Pare and core one fresh pineapple and cut in bite-size chunks. You should have about 4 cups. Refrigerate.

At serving time, divide the pineapple among 8 low individual serving dishes. Combine 1 8-oz. container of sour cream with 2 T. brown sugar and ⅛ t. nutmeg. Spoon the sour cream onto the pineapple chunks and sprinkle each serving with about ½ t. brown sugar (additional).

8 servings.

Mama's Apple Macaroon

In a greased 9-inch pie plate, place 3½ C. sliced apples (enough to heap up in center). Sprinkle apples with ½ C. sugar and ½ t. cinnamon mixed together. Spread over all a batter made of:

1 C. sugar
½ C. butter
1 egg, beaten
2/3 C. flour
½ t. baking powder

Bake in a 350-degree oven for 35 to 40 minutes, or until apples are tender and cakelike crust is brown. May be served with whipped cream, if desired.

Makes 6 servings, cut in wedges.

Carol's Pineapple Cheese Cake With Apricot Sauce

Crust:
Combine the following ingredients, blend well, reserving ½ for topping:

2 C. graham cracker crumbs
2 C. vanilla wafers, crumbed
6 T. soft butter

In the bottom of a 9- by 9-inch pan, place half the crumb mixture, pressing down firmly.

Filling:
Drain 1 20-oz. can (2½ C.) crushed pineapple and to the juice add 2 T. unflavored gelatin. Combine 3 egg yolks (reserving the whites in another bowl) with ¾ C. sugar and ¼ C. milk in a large saucepan, stirring constantly over *low* heat. When thickened, add pineapple juice and gelatin and stir until dissolved. Cool.

Stir in:
2 C. cottage cheese, drained and sieved
1 8-oz. pkg. cream cheese, softened
1¼ C. of the pineapple
(Reserve the rest of the pineapple for the sauce.)

Beat the reserved egg whites until they form soft peaks, not dry. Fold into the pineapple-cheese mixture. Pour into the crumb-lined pan and sprinkle with the remaining half of the crumbs. Chill overnight. Cut into squares and serve with Apricot-Pineapple Sauce.

Sauce:
Mix 1¼ C. crushed pineapple with 1½ C. apricot nectar, 1 T. lemon juice, 1 T. cornstarch, ⅛ t. salt. Cook in a saucepan until thick. Chill and serve separately with Pineapple Cheese Cake.

Lemon Torte II

Combine in order given:
½ C. butter
½ C. sugar
3 eggs
½ t. vanilla
7 T. milk
1¼ C. cake flour sifted with
1 t. baking powder
⅛ t. salt

Pat mixture into an 8- or 9-inch spring-form pan and bake at 350 degrees until firm (about 20 minutes). Cool.

Filling:
Juice and rind of 1 lemon

Add:
1 C. sugar
2 egg yolks
1¼ C. warm water
3 T. cornstarch

Combine lemon, sugar, egg yolks, water, and cornstarch and cook over medium heat until thick and smooth. Spread over baked cake crust.

Cover all with a meringue made of:
the 3 egg whites *plus*
2 egg whites

gradually beat in 1 C. sugar. Sprinkle with:
½ C. chopped walnuts

Bake at 275 degrees for ½ hour.

Makes 10 to 12 servings.

So simple!

Sherbet Oranges

Cut in two as many oranges as you need for ½ orange per serving. Scoop out pulp and juice (to use for breakfast!) and cut a zigzag pattern at top of each half. Freeze the orange shell. When frozen, fill with orange, lime or lemon sherbet. Freeze until serving time. Top each serving with a cherry on a pick!

Lemon Dainty

(Light and lemony! Everybody's favorite!) Cakelike top and custard below!

Combine:

¾ C. sugar

3 T. flour

3 T. butter

2 egg yolks, beaten

Mix well and add juice and grated rind of one lemon, ⅛ t. salt, and 1 C. milk. Beat the remaining 2 egg whites with ¼ C. sugar until they hold firm peaks, but not dry. Fold into the first mixture. Turn into a 1-qt. buttered baking dish, and place dish in a pan of hot water (about 1 inch up outside of dish). Bake in a 350-degree oven about 50 minutes or until nicely brown and set. Serve with whipped cream, if desired.

Serves 6.

FISH & SEAFOOD

The variety of fish and seafood on the market today is endless. There are so many flavors that there should be many that appeal to you and your family. Frozen fish and seafood may be used in any of the following dishes. Fish and seafoods are delicate and never should be overcooked or you'll come up with mush. Shrimp and lobster become tough when overcooked, so easy does it! Here are some of the best from my collection!

Shrimp and Scallop Gruyere

(Best seafood dish I ever tasted!)

In a large saucepan melt ¾ C. butter. Add ¾ C. flour and stir until well blended, over medium heat. Add 3 C. milk and stir constantly until thickened, then add the following:

9 oz. Swiss Gruyere cheese, sliced thin
(Look for Swiss Gruyere in little wheels at the cheese department. They come in 6-oz. packages, wrapped in 1-oz. sections. This recipe takes 1½ pkgs.)
¼ t. garlic powder
2 t. salt
¼ t. pepper
¼ t. Accent
¼ t. dry mustard
1 T. tomato paste
2 t. lemon juice

In another saucepan, saute:
½ lb. fresh mushrooms in
2 T. butter

Cook, stirring carefully, 5 minutes. Add mushrooms to the sauce. In the same pan you have cooked the mushrooms, poach in 1 C. water 1 12-oz. pkg. frozen scallops for 5 minutes. Add to the sauce with ½ C. of the poaching broth. To the remaining broth, add 1 lb. fresh-frozen, cleaned, and deveined shrimp. Add shrimp to sauce. Now carefully stir all ingredients together. Serve in a chafing dish, piping hot, over steamed white rice.

Serves 6. So rich and satisfying!

Shrimp Creole I

In a large saucepan, saute in 2 T. fat:

1 medium green pepper, diced
1 medium onion, diced

Add:
1 No. 2 can tomatoes
1 small can tomato paste
1 paste can of water (rinse)
1 4-oz. can mushroom pieces
1 t. sugar
2 t. Gumbo file (Spice Islands)

Cook sauce slowly, stirring occasionally until it is the consistency of gravy (about 30 minutes). Add 1 No. 2 can cut okra and cook 10 minutes longer.

Add 1 lb. raw, cleaned shrimp; cook 5 minutes or until shrimp turn pink and edges curl.

Serve over white rice, steaming hot.

Serves 4 generously.

Shrimp Creole II, Victorian Style

In a large saucepan, melt 1/3 C. butter. Add ¼ C. flour and stir together over medium heat until the flour begins to brown lightly. Remove from heat and add 1¼ C. canned beef or chicken consomme. Blend well and cook over medium heat until slightly thickened.

In another pan, saute in 2 T. butter:

½ C. chopped onion
½ C. chopped green pepper
2 cloves garlic, crushed
¼ C. parsley, minced

Cook gently until vegetables are tender but not brown. Add:

1 8-oz. can tomato sauce
1 3-oz. can mushrooms
1 slice lemon
1 pkg. frozen baby okra
1 t. Gumbo file
2 dashes tabasco
1 bay leaf

and cook all together with the ingredients in the first saucepan, over low heat about 20 minutes. Remove bay leaf and lemon slice. Add 1 lb. raw, cleaned shrimp. Cook 5 minutes or until shrimp turns pink. Turn off heat and allow flavors to mingle about an hour (or can be made ahead!). At serving time: Heat *only* until mixture comes to a boil. Serve over white, fluffy rice.

Serves 4 scrumptiously!

Wild Rice-Seafood Supreme

Cook 2 pkg. Wild Rice-White Rice mixture according to package directions. Reserve.

Saute in 3 T. butter:

1 C. celery, diced
1 small onion, minced
3 T. green pepper, diced
1 3-oz. can mushroom pieces
½ of a 2-oz. jar of pimentos
½ t. salt
¼ t. pepper

When the vegetables are tender, but not brown, add 1 6-oz. pkg. frozen crabmeat (or 2 5½-oz. cans crabmeat, rinsed and drained) and 1 12-oz. pkg. frozen shrimp, cleaned and 1 can mushroom soup, undiluted. Cook 5 minutes. Combine with the precooked rice (about 4 C.) and turn into a buttered 2-qt. casserole. Bake at 350 degrees for 30 to 40 minutes.

Serves 8.

Fish Fillets in Mushroom-Wine Sauce

Melt 3 T. butter and stir in 3 T. flour, blending well. Add 1 can cream of mushroom soup mixed with 2/3 C. dry white wine. Stirring constantly, cook until thickened.

In a shallow baking dish, arrange:

1 to 1 1/3 lbs. raw fish fillets
(sole, cod, halibut, or flounder)

over the fillets, pour the sauce, and sprinkle with 3 T. grated Parmesan cheese and 2 T. chopped parsley. Bake at 375 degrees for 25 minutes or until fish flakes easily with a fork.

Fish Loaf with Mustard Sauce

Pour:
2/3 C. hot milk over
2 C. soft white bread crumbs

Add:
2 eggs, beaten
2 C. flaked fish (salmon, tuna, or precooked fillets)
1 T. onion, minced
1 T. parsley, minced
1 t. salt
⅛ t. pepper
2 T. soft butter

Mix all ingredients well, and press firmly into a greased loaf pan. Set loaf pan in a pan of hot water and bake at 350 degrees for 50 minutes. Allow to stand 5 minutes. Turn out on a hot platter, garnish with parsley and lemon wedges and pass the:

Mustard Sauce

Melt 2 T. butter in a saucepan and add 2 T. flour and stir until blended. Add 1¾ C. milk. Cook over medium heat until thick. Add ¼ C. prepared mustard and ½ t. salt. Blend well. Serve hot in a separate sauce bowl with the Fish Loaf. Elegant!

Berkley's Clam Sauce for Spaghetti

In a saucepan, heat 2 T. olive oil.

Add:
1 clove garlic, crushed
½ t. salt
⅛ t. pepper
¼ t. oregano
1 T. parsley, minced

Add:
1 10½-oz. can minced clams
1 8-oz. can baby whole clams
Liquid from both cans of clams
2 T. cornstarch, stirred into clam juice

Heat slowly (preferably in top of chafing dish) until thoroughly heated. Serve over 8 oz. thin spaghetti, cooked according to package directions.

Serves 4.

Lobster-Ham Newburg

In a saucepan (or chafing dish) combine:

1 can cream of mushroom soup
1 can cream of chicken soup
1 can (4-oz.) button mushrooms
1 T. lemon juice
¼ t. paprika
1 T. parsley, minced
1 2-oz. jar pimento, chopped
½ C. pitted, ripe olives, sliced
1 C. ham, slivered
1 6-oz. can lobster meat, diced

Heat thoroughly. Serve over fluffy white rice.

Serves 4 to 6.

Baked Oyster Loaf

Chop on a board, with sharp knife:

1 pt. fresh or frozen small oysters

Add:
¾ lb. ground veal
¾ lb. lean, unseasoned ground pork
½ t. poultry seasoning
1 t. salt
¾ C. soft bread crumbs
1 egg, beaten

Mix thoroughly. Pack firmly into a loaf tin. Bake at 350 degrees for 1 hour, basting occasionally with melted butter (about 3 T. butter, melted). A perfect partner for this dish is "My Best Scalloped Potatoes!"

Perfect Deviled Crab

In a saucepan, melt 2 T. butter.

Add:
2 T. onion, minced
2 T. green pepper, minced
1 T. parsley, minced

Saute until vegetables are tender, but not brown. Stir in:

1 C. soft bread crumbs
½ C. undiluted celery soup
½ C. mayonnaise
1 T. catsup
1 t. worchestershire sauce
½ t. horseradish
½ t. prepared mustard

Rinse and drain well 2 cans (7¾-oz.) crab meat; pick out any cartilage and discard. Mix the crab meat with 3 T. lemon juice and toss well. Add to the sauce and blend well. Divide the mixture between 8 large baking shells (or 8 small individual baking ramekins) and sprinkle tops with a mixture of:

2 T. melted butter
¼ C. dry bread crumbs
¼ C. grated Parmesan cheese

Bake at 350 degrees for 20 minutes or until piping hot.

Serves 8.

Shrimps in Velvet

(Quick and fabulous for unexpected company!)

Thaw a 1½-lb. package of cleaned, deveined shrimp and saute in 1/3 C. butter for 2 minutes. Add ½ lb. fresh mushrooms, cleaned and sliced (or 1 4-oz. can mushroom buttons, sliced in two). Saute together for 3 minutes.

Add:

1½ C. sour cream

½ t. salt

2 t. soy sauce

½ t. paprika

Stir gently, over low heat, until sauce and seasonings blend and shrimp is hot. (Do not boil or the sour cream will separate!) Divide equally into four individual casseroles and dust with Parmesan cheese. Set under the broiler to glaze (watch carefully all the time) and serve toast points stuck in around the edge of casseroles.

Serves 4.

Marie's Lobster Thermidor

In a large frying pan, saute in ½ lb. butter:

1½ green peppers, chopped
1 whole pimento, diced
1 4-oz. can mushroom pieces

Saute 5 minutes and sprinkle with:
½ C. flour

Stir to blend well, then add 4 C. milk which have been blended with 3 beaten egg yolks. Cook until thickened and well blended. Add the diced meat from 5 or 6 lobster tails, thawed and cooked according to package directions. Turn all ingredients into a 2-qt. casserole and sprinkle with ¼ C. grated Parmesan cheese and a light dusting of paprika. Bake at 300 degrees for 50 to 60 minutes. Serve on hot buttered toast points.

Serves 6.

Salmon in Sour Cream

Drain a 1-lb. can Red Sockeye Salmon, remove bones and skin, and separate the meat into bite-size chunks.

Combine:
2 T. green onion, minced fine
1 t. parsley, minced
¼ t. rosemary leaves, crumbled
½ t. salt
⅛ t. pepper (freshly ground is best)
1 C. sour cream
2 T. mayonnaise

Turn the sauce over the salmon chunks and toss lightly with a fork. Chill an hour or so. Garnish with parsley and lemon wedges.

Serves 4.

Scallop Kebobs

Thaw 1 lb. frozen scallops and marinate in 3 T. lemon juice for 30 minutes. Drain.

On 6 long skewers, alternate the scallops with pineapple chunks (about 2 C.), a green pepper cut in 12 chunks, and about 12 red cherry tomatoes. Broil about 10 minutes, basting with melted butter once or twice. Do not turn as tomatoes are too fragile. Sprinkle lightly with salt and a little freshly ground pepper.

Serves 6.

Colorado Mountain Trout

In a heavy skillet, combine:
3 T. salad oil
1 T. bacon fat
1 T. butter

Stir gently to combine the fats. When fat is hot, not smoking, dip well-cleaned trout in a shallow pan containing about ½ to 1 C. milk, then into cornmeal (about ½ C. spread out on a waxed paper), then into flour. Lay trout gently into the hot fat and turn several times as they cook, until meat flakes with a fork at the back of the fish—about 15 to 30 minutes, depending on the size of the trout. Salt lightly. Serve with lemon wedges on a bed of watercress, if you can!

To bone trout perfectly, slit skin to the bone along the back. With a table knife in one hand and a fork in the other, gently run knife along rib cage of trout and lift off the meat on top side, lay back, flesh side up with the fork and knife as a tong, lift off the skeleton and the lower side of the fish will be free of bones.

FOREIGN COOKERY

You will find that nothing is so rewarding as planning and preparing a dinner with a real foreign accent. Most of the recipes are tailored for American taste and availability of materials. When you choose the kind of food you want to serve, try to complete the picture with table decor suitable to the country. Often you can find pictures, in books of the particular country, to give you ideas—or be original. Just an item or two, such as a flower arrangement or a particular type of candleholder or napkins, is enough to remind your family and guests that you had lots of fun preparing the meal. You know, that's the feeling you want to impart—that you cared enough to have it all really perfect—for them!

Mexican

Ever since we moved to Colorado, we have had a great interest in the Spanish-American people, their language, and their marvelous food. Those of you who have never experimented with this cookery have an unusual treat in store—don't be afraid of it! Most of the recipes are really mild in flavor.

Chili Con Queso (Cheese with Chili Peppers)

A dip for king-size corn chips.

In the top of a double boiler, over simmering water, melt together:

1 lb. Velveeta cheese
1 3-oz. can (hot or mild) drained green chili peppers, diced
1 3-oz. can pimentos, diced
Liquid from can of pimentos
1 t. chili powder
½ t. garlic powder
1 C. solid pack tomatoes, drained and chopped

Combine and serve warm with king-size corn chips or tostados. Makes about 3 cups.

To make tostados: Cut canned or frozen tortillas in fourths and fry crisp in hot salad oil. Drain and salt lightly.

Mexican Noodles, Colorado Style (A casserole dish)

In 2 T. salad oil, saute

1½ lbs. smoked ham, ground
with
½ C. onion, diced

2 T. green pepper, diced

When vegetables are tender, turn off heat and add ½ lb. cheddar cheese, diced and

1 No. 2 can tomatoes
1 No. 2 can green peas, drained
1 2-oz. jar pimentos, diced
1 t. paprika
1 t. salt
½ t. pepper
1 8-oz. pkg. noodles, cooked

Combine all ingredients and mix gently. Bake in a 2-qt. casserole at 350 degrees for 50 to 60 minutes.

Serves about 8. Mild flavor! Delicious!

Enchiladas Con Pollo (Chicken Enchiladas)

12 6- or 8-inch tortillas

Sauce:
In a medium size saucepan, saute:

½ C. onion diced and
1 large clove of garlic, crushed in
2 T. olive oil (or salad oil)

Add:

1½ green peppers, diced
3 large green chili peppers, cut

Turn the above ingredients into a blender and chop until well blended and smooth. Return to the pan and add:

2 T. parsley, minced fine
½ t. salt
1 not-too-ripe tomato, diced fine
1½ C. sour cream
2 T. sesame seeds, browned in:
1 t. butter

Now you will need the meat from a 2-lb. cooked chicken, finely shredded (about 3 C.), 2 C. grated cheddar cheese, ½ C. sliced ripe olives, and ½ small head of lettuce, shredded—all on separate pieces of waxed paper.

Method: Heat about 1 C. salad oil in an electric fry pan until control light goes out at 375 degrees. With a tong, pass each of the 12 large tortillas (canned or frozen and thawed) through the hot fat only to soften. Do not crisp! Put each one on a waxed paper until you have finished. (Turn off heat on fry pan.) Dip each tortilla in a bit of chicken broth to moisten (about ¾ C.). Divide the shredded chicken among the 12 tortillas (about ¼ C. on each) and cover with 2 T. of the sauce on each. Sprinkle with a bit of the green onion, sliced olives, and lettuce. Roll each tortilla around the filling and place, fold down, in a shallow baking dish. Cover with remaining sauce and sprinkle with the grated cheese. Bake at 350 degrees for 30 minutes or until cheese is melted and slightly brown and bubbly! (Mild and very authentic!) By the way, if any chicken broth from the dipping is left, you may turn it into the baking pan around the tortillas, to use it up!

Quick Tamale Pie

(So easy—so good!)

Into a 1½-qt. casserole, place the following ingredients, in layers:

1 No. 2 can chili with beans
1 No. 2 can whole kernel corn, drained
1 small clove garlic, crushed
1 small can chopped ripe olives
1 medium onion, diced fine
1 can tamales, cut in 1-inch pieces

(Do not use the fat in the can of tamales—discard!)

Sprinkle the top with ½ C. grated cheddar cheese and bake at 350 degrees for 45 minutes.

Serves 6.

Guacamole Salad (Avocado)

Mash 2 large ripe avocados, peeled and seeded in a medium size bowl. Put a large clove of garlic through a garlic press (or mince finely) and add to avocados.

Add:

3 small green onions, minced

1 large tomato, diced

¼ t. salt

Several grinds of fresh pepper

Mix well. If it is necessary to let stand until serving time, sprinkle top with a little lemon juice to prevent discoloration. Serve in a lettuce cup.

Serves 4.

Mexican Coffee

(Delish!)

Perk a 6-cup pot of coffee, using 10 coffee spoons of coffee for extra strength.

In a large pan, combine 6 cups whole milk, 1 C. Hersey's chocolate syrup, 1 T. cinnamon and bring to boiling point. Do not boil!

When coffee is perked, pour into the pan with the milk mixture. Pour into a heated serving pot and serve to the "oohs and ahs" of your family and guests!

Gazpacho
(Cold soup and a fine appetizer)

Combine:

2 cans (10½-oz.) beef consomme
2 cans (5¼-oz.) tomato or vegetable cocktail juice
¼ C. lemon juice
½ t. salt
1 clove garlic, pressed
2 large tomatoes, chopped
1 medium cucumber, chopped
3 T. green onions, minced
3 T. green pepper, minced
1 T. pimento, diced
1 t. paprika
2 T. olive oil
½ t. worchestershire sauce
Freshly ground black pepper

Let stand at room temperature about 1 hour. Then chill at least two hours. Serve, topped with a few croutons, in soup bowls or glass fruit dishes.

Serves 6.

Huevos Rancheros (Eggs, Ranch Style—famous!)

Finely chop 1 large green chili (canned). Combine with 1 medium onion, chopped, 1 clove garlic (pressed), and 1 C. tomato, diced fine. Place ingredients in a saucepan and add ½ t. sugar, 1 t. salt, 1 T. dried parsley, crumbled, and a pinch of oregano. Bring to a boil and simmer gently 5 minutes.

In a frying pan, heat 2 T. butter and break 6 eggs into it; add 2 t. water around eggs and, cooking at low temperature about 300 to 325 degrees, cook until eggs are set. Serve on warm platter with the sauce poured over eggs. Garnish with parsley and serve with crisp tostadas.

Serves 3 to 6.

Old Spanish Style Tacos

(The method is age-old, but not the method currently used. I was taught to make these by Rose Medina who with her husband owns and operates the Wagon Wheel Restaurant in San Luis, Colorado. Don't miss this place if your travels take you within 100 miles!)

The filling:
1 lb. lean hamburger browned in
1 T. salad oil with
½ t. salt and
½ t. garlic salt

To this add:
1 T. flour and
3 T. taco sauce and

cook until thickened. Have ready:

½ C. grated cheddar cheese
1 C. fresh tomatoes, diced fine
½ small head lettuce, shredded

(This amount will fill about 6 *tortillas*, generously, but you better make twice the recipe!)

Method:
Soften the tortillas in a small amount of fat and fill the center with the meat mixture, holding so you may fold the tortilla in two; sprinkle with a bit of cheese and fold together. On a hot griddle, brown and crisp the tortilla with the filling inside. When crisp, open a little way and sprinkle in a bit of the tomato and lettuce. Refold and serve with Taco Sauce:

Taco Sauce de Medina

1 T. hot, dried, crushed red chili peppers
1 C. tomato juice

In a jar which will hold a cup and a half of liquid, pour the tomato juice and add the chili peppers. Shake vigorously. Let stand at least a day. Shake again. Serve separately, to be spooned or poured into taco shell. Easy does it!

"Island" Dishes

Especially since Hawaii became one of our own beautiful states, it makes us more aware of the fine things they offer us, including succulent dishes such as the recipes below. Why not try a Hawaiian luau? Most of the preparation can be made the day before your party—have several dishes, lots of white fluffy rice, and a simple dessert, and you'll be called *wonderful*!

Hawaiian Pork

Cut 1½ lbs. lean pork into ½-inch strips.
Beat until smooth:
1 egg
1 T. milk
1 T. flour
¼ t. salt

Dip the pork strips in the batter and saute in 3 T. fat until brown.

Cook:
1 clove garlic, pressed, in
1 T. salad oil

Add:
1 chicken boullion cube
1 C. water
1 C. pineapple tidbits
½ C. pineapple juice
1 thinly sliced carrot
2 T. soy sauce
2 T. wine vinegar
1 T. sugar
1 medium green pepper, cut in strips

Simmer 5 minutes. Add meat. Thicken with 3 t. cornstarch mixed with a little water. Serve with rice.

Serves 4.

Yam-Ban Bake

In a shallow baking pan 9 x 13 inches, slice in ½-inch slices 4 large yams. Over the yams, pour a mixture of:

¾ C. undiluted frozen orange juice
2 T. grated onion
¼ C. brown sugar, packed firm
¼ t. nutmeg
2 T. peach or apricot jam
½ t. salt

Cover pan with foil. Bake at 350 degrees for 1 hour or until potatoes are fork tender.

Peel and halve, lengthwise, 4 bananas (not too ripe). Place bananas on top of yams and baste bananas with juice in pan. Dot bananas with butter and return to oven 10 minutes more. Do not cover so bananas will glaze. (Baste with juices, if necessary!)

A beautiful accompaniment to a luau can be made by choosing a fresh pineapple with nice leaves at the top. Wash the pineapple using a brush. Arrange, in rows, vertically—small cauliflowerettes, radishes, black and green olives, and cherry tomatoes impaled on cocktail picks. Serve with your choice of dips, such as avocado or a cream cheese dip.

Pork Bundles with Curry-Ginger Sauce

(You won't be disappointed in this!)

Cut 2 lbs. of pork tenderloin in: julienne strips and brown in 1 T. fat. Sprinkle strips with:

1½ t. salt

½ t. paprika

½ t. ground ginger

When well blended with meat, add ¼ C. water to pan and cover tightly. At low heat, cook 30 minutes or until meat is tender. Remove meat from pan into a medium size bowl. To the drippings in the pan add 1 C. canned chicken broth which has been mixed with 2 T. flour. Stir constantly until thickened; add to the gravy 1 C. mandarin orange slices (cut slices in two) and ¼ C. flaked coconut and the reserved pork strips. Toss together lightly until well mixed. Reserve for next step.

Wash 16 large romaine leaves (or more, if you need to overlap some leaves to make them large enough for the "bundle"). Pare the ridge on each leaf so it can be folded easily. Pour boiling water over the leaves and drain immediately. Divide the meat-fruit mixture between the leaves, putting filling at large end of leaf and folding around filling. Secure bundles with picks and place seam side down in a large baking pan. Cover and refrigerate about 2 hours.

In the meantime, prepare the curry-ginger sauce. In a small pan, saute 1 clove garlic, pressed, with ¼ C. finely diced onion in 2 T. butter. Add 2 t. curry powder. Cook until onions are tender but not brown. Add 1¼ C. chicken broth (canned is fine!) into which has been stirred 2 T. flour. Cook until it thickens, about 2 minutes. Remove from heat and add 2 T. chopped candied ginger. Serve some sauce over the bundles and to glaze—and the rest, in a bowl to pass.

To prepare the bundles: In a large roasting pan, put enough water to cover the pan to a depth of about 1 inch. Place the bundles on a wire rack (for a makeshift rack, use chicken wire or foil crumpled to support a foil pan—or invent your own; however, most roasters have a rack that can be supported), careful not to unfold, and steam 25 minutes. Serve on a warm platter with some of the sauce and a garnish of additional mandarin oranges (cold) and leaves of your choice (I use fern leaves!).

Polynesian Beef

Place a 3½- to 4-lb. beef chuck roast in a bowl and pour over it the following marinade:

1 C. pineapple juice
1 medium onion, sliced and separated into rings
3 T. soy sauce
1 t. ginger
½ t. salt

Let meat remain in marinade 2 hours. Remove meat and wipe with paper towels. Reserve the marinade.

In a heavy kettle, or Dutch oven, heat 2 T. salad oil and brown the meat lightly on both sides. Again cover with the marinade and simmer until fork-tender, about 1½ hours. When tender, add:

4 stalks of celery, sliced diagonally
4 carrots, sliced thin

and cook 10 minutes longer. Then add 4 large fresh mushrooms, sliced thin, and ½ lb. fresh spinach leaves, stems removed. Cover and cook 5 minutes.

Remove meat and vegetables to a warm platter. Keep hot and make gravy of pan juices by stirring in a little cornstarch which has been mixed with a small amount of cold water. Stir until slightly thickened and serve over the sliced meat.

German

Colorado is a state comprised mainly of nature-lovers who breathe happiest in the appetite-whetting mountain air. Whether they come in from skiing, fishing, or mountain hiking—or a trip to watch the birds—they're hungry! What can be so enjoyable as the smells that come from the kitchen where fragrant German cooking is being prepared? Let's give them a taste to remember with a few of the favorites from my files!

Sauerbraten

Rub a 4-lb. beef chuck (or round bone) roast with 2t. salt and 1 t. ginger and place in a gallon stone crock (or a deep bowl).

In a large saucepan, over medium heat, bring to a boil the following ingredients:

2 C. cider vinegar
2½ C. water
2 medium onions, sliced
2 T. mixed pickling spices
1 t. whole peppercorns
8 whole cloves
1/3 C. sugar

Boil 2 minutes and pour hot, over the meat. Allow to stand in a cool place (or refrigerate) for 3 or 4 days, turning once a day.

On preparation day, remove meat from marinade, wipe dry with paper towels, and brown in 2 T. hot bacon drippings. (Brown slowly over medium heat!) Reserve marinade. Add 1 C. marinade to browned meat and simmer slowly in a heavy kettle until tender—about 3 hours. Add liquid, if necessary. Remove meat to warm platter. Strain liquid. You should have about 2 C. of liquid in the pan. To this, add 6 or 8 *gingersnaps* (the 2-inch size) to thicken. Slice the meat thin and dribble the gravy over the meat. Serve with potato pancakes,* warm applesauce, sweet and sour red cabbage*, and apple streudel.

Serves 6.

*Recipes included in this book.

German Red Cabbage (Sweet and Sour)

Shred 1 medium head of red cabbage (about 3 lbs.) and place in a saucepan with:

2 tart cooking apples, peeled and sliced
1 small onion, diced
2 T. bacon fat
1 t. salt
¼ C. vinegar
¼ C. sugar
Freshly ground pepper

Cover and simmer about ½ hour or until cabbage is tender. Sprinkle with 1 T. flour and stir until thickened (1 t. caraway seeds may be added, if desired).

Serves 6.

Potato Pancakes

(I want to suggest using a blender for mixing the potato pancakes to prevent discoloration of the potatoes! If you don't have one, you may grind the potatoes and onion in a food chopper, but the product will be less perfect.)

In a blender, put 4 eggs and blend until fluffy—about 5 seconds. Add:

2/3 C. flour
1 t. salt
2 T. salad oil
½ C. milk
3 T. onion, cut up
2 C. diced raw potatoes (small dice)
1 t. lemon juice

Turn on blender again and blend about 5 seconds or until smooth. Bake in medium size pancakes on a greased hot griddle. Turn once. Do not stack pancakes. Makes 16 to 20 pancakes.

Potato Dumplings

Cook 6 medium potatoes until tender and force through a ricer onto a large platter. Let stand overnight, uncovered, to dry out. When cooking time arrives, put in a bowl (you should have about 4½ C.) and add:

½ C. flour
¼ C. farina (or cream of wheat, uncooked)
1 t. salt
2 eggs, slightly beaten
⅛ t. nutmeg
½ t. sugar

Mix well. Form into 8 or 10 balls. Have a large kettle of boiling water ready and add 1 t. salt. (Test one ball in the boiling water before you add them all to make sure there is enough flour in them, as flour varies—high altitude flours are recommended in Colorado. If ball appears not to be holding its form, add a small amount of flour to remaining balls.) Boil 20 minutes. Lift out with a slotted spoon and serve immediately with gravy made from your meat or with melted butter.

German Meatballs with Caraway

Coarsely grate 1 C. raw potatoes. Drain well.

Add:
1 lb. lean ground beef
1 t. salt
¼ t. pepper
1 T. minced parsley
½ t. grated onion
1 t. grated lemon peel
1 egg, slightly beaten

Mix well and form into 1½-inch balls. Dip in flour. Drop into 6½ C. boiling beef broth (homemade or canned). Simmer 30 minutes until tender. Remove meat to a covered serving dish. Keep warm. To the stock in the pan, add: ½ t. caraway seeds, 2 T. flour mixed with ¼ C. cold water, and some freshly ground pepper. Cook until lightly thickened, stirring constantly. Serve over the meatballs to 4 or 6.

Very good served with Potato Dumplings!

Hasenpfeffer

You won't be sorry you tried this delicious sweet-sour rabbit dish. Our friends really like this—serve Potato Pancakes and Red Cabbage.

1 large (or 2 small) rabbits, cleaned perfectly, and cut into serving pieces. Place rabbit in a stone crock or large bowl.

In a large saucepan, combine:

½ C. vinegar
½ C. water
1 onion, sliced
1 carrot, sliced
6 whole cloves
1 bay leaf
⅛ t. sage

Bring to a boil and pour over the rabbit. Allow to stand 2 or 3 days in the refrigerator—stir several times to distribute the seasonings. Drain well, reserving the marinade. Wipe meat with paper towels and brown slowly in a heavy kettle in 4 T. butter and 1 T. bacon fat. Add 1 C. marinade and simmer slowly 1 to 1½ hours, or until meat is fork-tender, adding more marinade as it evaporates. When meat is tender, remove to a hot platter and keep warm. Strain the liquid in the pan (there should be about 1½ C.—add some marinade if not enough liquid). To the liquid, add 3 T. flour mixed with ¼ C. water and stir constantly until thick. (Add more salt and pepper to taste.) Stir in 1 C. sour cream and bring to boiling point, but do *not* boil. Pour over the rabbit. Serve with a heap of rice and some currant jelly!

Serves 4.

Dorothy's Ham and Apples (With Dumplings!)

Cook a piece of ham weighing about 2½ to 3 lbs. for 1 hour, slowly, in 1 qt. water. When ham is tender, add to the pan one package (about 1¼ C.) dehydrated apple slices and ½ C. brown sugar. Continue cooking until apples are tender (about 35 minutes). To the ham and apples, add dumplings:

Sift 1 C. flour with 1½ t. baking powder and ¼ t. salt. Mix 1 beaten egg with ½ C. milk. Stir with egg-milk mixture, all at one time, into the flour. Stir only until flour is moistened. Drop by spoonfuls over boiling ham and apples. Cover tightly and do not lift cover for 15 minutes.

Serves 4.

Renie's Kraut Bierocks

Try this with a simple salad and a light dessert and you'll be delighted with this wonderful "sandwich" variation! (For a shortcut, in this recipe I suggest using a packaged hot roll mix.)

1 pkg. hot roll mix, prepared according to directions on package. Prepare this, and while it is raising, prepare the following:

In a bowl, mix:
1 lb. lean hamburger

1 egg

1 t. salt

⅛ t. pepper

In a large skillet, melt 2 T. fat and to it add 2 C. shredded cabbage and 1 T. diced onion. Stir and fry a few minutes until cabbage starts to become limp. Add the meat mixture and stir and cook until redness has gone from the meat. Turn off heat and cool slightly.

Roll out the roll mix into a thin sheet and cut in 3½-inch squares. On each square place some of the meat mixture (about 3 T.). Fold the dough around the filling and press to seal the edges. Put rolls on a greased cookie sheet and allow to raise 20 to 30 minutes. Bake at 350 degrees for 20 to 25 minutes or until nicely browned. Brush tops with melted butter and enjoy, enjoy!

Serves 4 to 6, depending on appetite! This amount should make about 8 or 10 rolls.

Hungarian

Paprikash (For a Crowd!)

Brown 3 lbs. beef, cut in cubes, in ¼ C. fat, in a heavy Dutch oven. When richly brown on all sides, add:

5 onions, sliced thin
1 t. dry mustard
2 t. salt
¼ C. brown sugar
3 t. paprika
4 T. worchestershire sauce
2 t. vinegar
¼ C. catsup
1½ C. water
1½ C. red, dry wine

Cover tightly and simmer slowly 2 to 2½ hours or until meat is very tender. Add ¼ C. flour to enough water to make a thin paste (about ½ C.) and stir into the liquid in the pan. Stir until thickened. Add 1 C. sour cream and stir until well blended and hot, but do *not* boil after cream is added. Serve over rice or noodles.

Serves 8.

Oriental

What is more exotic than beautiful Oriental food? Every offering is a work of art: garnishes of the simplist nature, carrot slices cut like flower petals, little triangles of green pepper, even tiny spinach leaves in a clear broth make the eye appeal as wonderful as the flavor. I offer you now the very best of my huge collection, and I do hope you will enjoy making them as much as I have.

Beautiful Egg Drop Soup (For Your First Course)

Have 6 C. clear chicken broth (canned or homemade) boiling rapidly. Beat 2 eggs slightly. Turn heat under broth to simmer. Quickly *stirring* broth, add the egg slowly. Add ½ C. finely shredded, deveined spinach leaves. Remove from heat. Season with 1 t. soy sauce.

Serves 8.

Purple Plum Duckling

This is my most prized Oriental recipe! The sauce is excellent on other fowl, also, but do try it my way the first time. You'll receive an encore!

You will need 2 5- to 6-lb. ducklings to serve 6 people. Have your butcher cut the birds in 4 pieces each. (If frozen, he can saw them in 4.) Thaw, if frozen. Rub inside and outside with a bit of onion and garlic salts. In a shallow roasting pan, set each quarter-bird on a "trivet" made of a thick slice of unpeeled orange. Place in an oven set at 350 degrees for 1½ hours, until brown and the fat has melted off. Remove from oven and drain off all fat in pan. Pull orange slices into the open now and brush both duckling and orange slices with Purple Plum Sauce:

Purple Plum Sauce

Cook 1 medium onion, diced in ¼ C. butter until tender, but not browned. Add:

1 17-oz. can purple plums, drained, pitted, and pureed
1 6-oz. can frozen lemonade
1/3 C. chili sauce
¼ C. soy sauce
1 t. worchestershire sauce
1 t. ginger
2 t. prepared mustard
2 drops Tabasco

Simmer all together 15 minutes. Coat duckling and oranges with the sauce every ten minutes for a period of half an hour, lowering oven temperature to 325 degrees. (Total baking time is 2 hours.)

Serves 6.

Steak and Pepper Chow Mein

(Assemble all ingredients and keep in separate bowls and this meal can be made in minutes!)

Cook in 2 T. salad oil, a 1½-lb. slice of top sirloin steak—to rare degree of doneness—browning on both sides. Remove from heat to a slicing board and slice thinly into 1-inch strips. Place strips in a deep bowl and sprinkle with 3 T. soy sauce. Allow to stand until you are ready to assemble the dish. Brown 1 T. sesame seeds in pan in which you cooked the meat. Reserve. Add 3 T. salad oil to the pan and when hot, saute 1 C. diagonally sliced celery and ¼ C. sliced green onions. Stir-fry gently for 5 minutes. Add 1 clove garlic, pressed, and 1 large green pepper cut in narrow strips. Saute 2 minutes. (Color of vegetables must remain vivid and texture must be tender-crisp.) Add the beef strips and marinade. Blend 2 T. cornstarch with 1 C. chicken broth, and ¼ t. powdered ginger (or fresh ginger root, grated*). Stir into simmering meat and vegetables—boil 1 minute. Add the sesame seeds and 2 medium size tomatoes, diced. Toss lightly. Serve in a heated bowl with hot fluffy rice (separately).

Makes 4 servings. Extra special!

*When you find fresh ginger root, buy several pieces. Peel, cut into pieces about the size of a walnut. Put in a covered jar and freeze. You need not thaw to grate what you need.

Oriental Mushroom-Chicken

Combine:
1 T. soy sauce
1 t. cornstarch
½ t. salt
¼ t. pepper
2 T. salad oil

Pour this mixture over 6 double chicken breasts (12 halves). Rub in well and marinate 30 minutes. Remove breast bones, if not already done, and *tear* the meat into shreds from ¼ to ½ inch wide and as long as they will tear conveniently.

Heat 2 T. salad oil with 1 large clove of garlic, pressed, and a dollar-size slice of fresh ginger root, grated. Saute 3 minutes and add torn chicken breasts.

In the meantime, heat 1 6-oz. can mushrooms and juice with 2 t. cornstarch and ¼ t. salt. Stir until thickened. Pour over the chicken breasts and stir. Fry until meat is white and curled. Do not overcook. Serve over white fluffy rice.

Serves 6.

Cantonese Pork

"Make ahead" Sauce: In a saucepan, combine:

1 11-oz. can tomato sauce
1 C. unsweetened pineapple juice
3 T. cornstarch
¼ C. sugar
¼ C. soy sauce
½ C. dry sherry

Cook until thickened, about 30 minutes. Add 2 T. wine vinegar. Remove from heat and pour over the pork and vegetables, prepared in the following manner:

Cut 2 lbs. boneless, lean pork shoulder in bite-size pieces. Combine ¼ C. cornstarch and ½ t. salt and sprinkle over meat, tossing lightly. Sprinkle with 2 T. soy sauce and mix until evenly moist. In a heavy fry pan, saute the meat in 2 T. hot salad oil, over medium heat, turning until well browned and crisp, about 20 or 30 minutes. Transfer to a hot platter and keep warm. Remove all but 1 T. of fat from fry pan and add 1 large onion, cut in wedges and separated into "flower petals" and 1 green pepper, cut in strips. Stir-fry 2 minutes; do not brown. Arrange peppers and onions over the meat and garnish with 3 small tomatoes, cut in wedges. Pour sauce over all!

Serve to 6 hungry people.

Egg Foo Yung

Combine:

¾ C. cooked, chopped chicken, shrimp, pork, or crab
1 8-oz. can mushrooms, chopped and drained
1 green onion, minced
½ stalk celery, minced
½ of a No. 2 can bean sprouts, drained
¼ t. salt

Beat 4 eggs slightly and add to the above combination. Stir well. Cook in little "pancakes" on a hot, greased skillet. Serve with Chinese Brown Sauce:

In a saucepan, combine:

1½ C. chicken broth
2 T. cornstarch
1 t. soy sauce
¼ t. sugar
¼ t. salt

Cook until thickened and serve over Egg Foo Yung. Garnish with a light scattering of chopped green onion tops.

Wonderful for 4 people!

Oriental Sundae Sauce (For Ice Cream)

Combine:
1/3 C. light corn syrup
¼ C. finely diced, candied ginger
Dash of salt
¼ C. light cream

Simmer for 5 minutes and add another ¼ C. light cream, stirring in gradually. Heat thoroughly, but do *not* boil. Remove from heat. Stir in: ¼ C. butter and ½ t. vanilla. Serve warm (not hot) over vanilla ice cream. Makes ¾ C. of sauce.

Sweet and Pungent Shrimp

Cut 2 large green peppers in rings. Slice 2 onions in rings. Cook peppers and onions in boiling water until tender-crisp (about 5 or 6 minutes). Drain.

In a large fry pan, saute 1½ lbs. cleaned and deveined shrimp in 2 T. salad oil, until shrimp is pink and slightly curled (about 8 to 10 minutes, depending on size of shrimp. Do not overcook!). Remove shrimp to a warm platter. To the pan juices, add 1 C. chicken stock, 4 slices pineapple, cut in wedges, and the green pepper and onion rings. Cook 3 minutes. Stir in 4 T. cornstarch which has been mixed with ½ C. wine vinegar, ½ C. sugar, and 2 t. soy sauce. Cook only until thickened. Pour sauce over shrimp and serve with white fluffy rice.

Serves 4 to 6.

Italian

Thoughts of Italian food bring to mind a picture of red and white checked tablecloths, wine bottles with candles, violin music, and happy faces. Why don't you promote a real Italian party? Complete the picture-your way—but try some of these luscious, easy recipes.

Chana's Italian Chicken Livers (Different!)

In a heavy fry pan, cook 5 or 6 strips of bacon, diced, until crisp. Remove from pan and reserve. Remove all but 2 T. fat from pan. In the pan, saute ½ lb. chicken livers to medium rare. Remove from pan and reserve. To the pan add 1 clove garlic, pressed, and ¼ C. onion, chopped, and saute slightly. Add:

1 T. chopped parsley
1 6-oz. can tomato paste
1 C. water
½ t. salt
¼ t. pepper
1 3½-oz. can mushroom pieces

Simmer 20 minutes.

Five minutes before serving time, add the chicken livers to the sauce and simmer slowly until well heated. Serve over noodles or homemade Fettucine (below). Garnish with bacon pieces and sprinkle with grated Romano cheese (about ¼ C.).

Fettucine

In a medium bowl, put 2 C. sifted flour; sprinkle with 1 t. salt.

In another bowl, combine 2 eggs, slightly beaten, and ½ C. pureed spinach (baby food). Mix well.

Make a "well" in the flour and add the liquid all at once, mixing—first with a fork, then with the hand. Place ½ C. flour on a board and turn the dough onto it. Knead until all flour is used; add more, if needed, so as not to be sticky. When smooth and elastic, divide into 2 balls. Let rest on board, covered with a towel, for 1 hour to relax. Roll out as thinly as possible on a lightly floured board into rectangles approximately 14 inches x 16 inches. Roll up like a jelly roll and slice into ¼-inch strips. Unroll and spread out on board to dry a bit (about 2 hours). Boil in slightly salted water until tender, about 15 or 20 minutes. The noodles should not be overcooked, but a bit chewy (al dente). Makes about 1 lb. of noodles. Especially good with chicken livers or meatballs and sauce!

Italian Spaghetti Sauce

(In all my years of collecting recipes and searching for perfection of an Italian Tomato Sauce, this is my choice.)

In a heavy saucepan, combine:

¼ C. olive oil
1 C. chopped onion
1 clove garlic, pressed

Saute onion and garlic in oil until limp. Add:

1 2-lb., 3-oz. can Italian style tomatoes
1 6-oz. can tomato paste
1½ C. water (rinse paste can with it)
1 t. dried parsley or 3 springs fresh parsley
1 t. salt
2 t. sugar
1 t. dried oregano
½ t. dried basil
Fresh ground pepper

Bring to a boil, reduce heat, and simmer slowly, covered, stirring occasionally about 1½ hours or until thick. Makes about 6 cups of sauce.

Gourmet Meatballs

Combine:
1 lb. ground beef
1 lb. ground veal
1 C. soft bread crumbs
¼ C. onion, minced fine
¼ C. grated Romano cheese
2 T. parsley
½ t. basil
1 egg
1½ t. salt
⅛ t. pepper
¼ C. beef boullion

Mix thoroughly. Form into small balls. Brown lightly and add to Italian Sauce about 30 minutes before serving time. Serve on top of spaghetti, with sauce and a light sprinkle of Romano cheese. Makes about 20 meatballs.

Chicken Cacciatore

Cut 2 2½-lb. to 3-lb. fryers into serving pieces and brown in 2 T. butter and 2 T. salad oil. When nicely browned, remove chicken from pan and reserve. To the pan juices, add:

1 C. onion, finely diced
¾ C. green pepper, diced
1 clove garlic, pressed

Saute lightly and add:

1 6-oz. can mushroom buttons
1 No. 2 can tomatoes (2½ C.)
1 8-oz. can tomato paste
½ C. Chianti wine (or water)
¾ t. salt
½ t. pepper
¼ t. allspice
½ t. dried thyme leaves, crushed
1 bay leaf

Simmer sauce 30 minutes. Place the chicken with the sauce in a covered baking dish and bake 30 minutes at 350 degrees. Serve with hot French bread and a tossed green salad with Italian style dressing. Yum!

Scandinavian

Selma's Norwegian Meatballs

In a medium size bowl, mix 1 lb. lean ground chuck with ½ t. salt and ¼ t. pepper.

In a saucepan, combine:

¼ C. onion, finely minced
1/3 C. hot water
½ t. B.V. extract (Wilson's)
⅛ t. basil
⅛ t. marjoram

Simmer over low heat for 5 minutes. Cool. Add 1 egg and mix well. Add ¼ C. finely crushed soda crackers, and ¼ C. quick-cooking oatmeal. Turn all into the bowl with the meat and mix well. Make into small balls, shaping on a teaspoon. Dredge lightly with flour and brown in a heavy fry pan, in 2 T. fat—takes about 12 to 15 minutes. Transfer meatballs to a covered casserole dish. To the brown bits in the fry pan, add 1 C. water, 1 t. B.V. extract. Stir well. Turn the liquid over the meatballs and cover. Bake at 325 degrees for 1 hour. At serving time, drain the juices from the casserole and thicken with a bit of flour (2 T. flour to 1 C. liquid).

Makes about 30 meatballs.

Mabel's Sweet Soup (Sot Supe)

Cover 1 lb. prunes and 1 lb. raisins with water enough to cover fruit. Let stand 2 hours. Bring slowly to a boil and cook until prunes are tender.

Add:
¾ C. sugar
Sliced rind and juice of ½ lemon
1 large stick of cinnamon

Cook 15 minutes on low heat.

Soak 1/3 C. minute tapioca in 1/3 C. water for 5 minutes and add to the fruit mixture. Cook slowly until tapioca is tender and sauce is thickened. Add ½ C. grape juice. Stir well.

Serve warm as a soup or cold as dessert.

Makes about 1 quart.

Scandinavian Supper Soup

In a heavy kettle, put 1 1-lb. package dried, split peas to soak in 6 C. boiling water. Cover. Let stand 1 hour. Bring to a boil, and cook slowly 1½ hours, with 2 lbs. sliced, smoked pork hocks and 1 T. dried onion flakes. When peas are tender, remove pork hocks and bones, and put the peas through a sieve or whirl in a blender until smooth. Cut the lean meat from the hocks and return to the peas.

Add:
2 carrots, peeled and diced
½ C. diced celery
1 T. parsley, minced
½ t. salt
¼ t. thyme
⅛ t. pepper
2 C. water

Simmer all together for 20 minutes, or until vegetables are tender. Add 1 whole Kielbasa sausage (weighing about 1 to 1½ lbs.). Simmer gently 20 minutes or more.

To serve, cut the sausage in serving pieces in each bowl with the soup. Serve with Swedish Rye bread and mustard, served separately.

Serves 6.

Danish Mon Tart

Beat together:
½ C. soft butter
½ C sugar

Add:
2 eggs, beating after each addition.

Add:
Grated rind of one lemon
4 t. lemon juice

Sift together:
1 C. sifted flour
1/3 t. salt

Add the flour gradually to the sugar and butter mixture. Turn into a buttered 9-inch spring-form pan.

On the top of the batter, arrange 4 medium size apples, peeled and sliced, which have been tossed with the remaining lemon juice. Drizzle 2 T. melted butter over the apple slices and sprinkle with ¼ C. sugar. Bake at 350 degrees for 1 hour or until the cake leaves the sides of the pan.

Serve warm with whipped cream and a *light* sprinkle of cinnamon.

Serves 8.

Roast Pork with Prunes

With a sharp, pointed knife, make 12 deep cuts in a center-cut pork loin roast (weighing about 3½ to 4 lbs.). Fill cuts with 12 ready-to-eat prunes, pushing them well into the meat. Combine 1 t. salt, ¼ t. pepper, and ½ t. ginger and rub into the roast. Put roast on a trivet or rack in a shallow roasting pan and roast about 2 hours (or until a meat thermometer indicates 185 degrees). When well done, remove meat to a warm platter.

Pour off all but ¼ C. of the fat in the pan and add 2 T. flour to the pan juice; stir until flour is browned a little. Remove from heat. Add 1 C. warm water and stir well. Return to heat, stirring constantly until thickened. Salt and pepper to taste. Add ¼ t. bottled gravey sauce (B.V.), ¼ C. light cream, and 1 T. applesauce. Serve gravy separately, along with boiled potatoes, a green salad, and cold applesauce.

Serves 6 to 8.

Danish Sugar-Fried Potatoes

In a heavy skillet, melt 4 T. butter and add 4 T. sugar, over medium heat. Stir constantly until the sugar has browned to a caramel color. Add 12 to 15 small, round, cooked potatoes (or canned), drained. Stir until potatoes are well coated. Reduce heat and thoroughly heat the potatoes. Sprinkle lightly with salt and a bit of chopped parsley.

Serves 6.

Aebleskiver (Apple Pancakes)

For this recipe, one needs an aebleskiver pan—with deep indentations to make individual cakes—they are lovely and very impressive for so simple a trick!

Separate 2 eggs and beat the whites stiff, but not dry, in a small bowl.

In a separate bowl, combine the 2 egg yolks with:

2 C. buttermilk
2 C. flour, sifted with:
1½ t. baking powder
½ t. soda
½ t. salt
2 T. sugar

Fold in the beaten egg whites while you are heating your aebleskiver pan. Pan is hot when a drop of water bounces on it. Rub ½ t. salad oil in each indentation and turn carefully to coat the pan. Put 1 T. batter in each indentation cup and on top of the batter put 1 t. thick applesauce; cover applesauce with another 1 T. bater. When the bottom part of the cake is cooked, take 2 forks and roll as a ball, onto the top. Cook until done and all batter has stopped bubbling—about 5 minutes. Serve with syrup or dusted with powdered sugar. Makes 15 to 20 cakes. So much fun after you practice a couple of pans full! (Oil the pan each time!)

French

Coq Au Vin Blanc (Chicken in White Wine)

1 4-lb. chicken (roasting type, if possible), cut in serving pieces. Brown the chicken pieces in ½ C. butter. Remove from pan into a covered 2-qt. casserole. In the remaining butter, saute:

½ lb. fresh mushrooms, sliced (or 1 large can mushrooms) (Reserve juice)
1 large onion, minced fine

Add to the chicken in the casserole and push down hard to pack the chicken parts together. Bake slowly, covered, for 1 hour at 325 degrees.

Remove the chicken from the casserole, leaving the onion and mushrooms. Add 1½ C. dry white wine, 1 C. chicken stock (part mushroom juice, if you have used canned mushrooms), and 2 T. flour. Mix well. Take out half this mixture. Return the chicken and pack down hard; return the second half of liquid and put cover on casserole. Bake 1 hour more, removing cover the last 15 or 20 minutes.

Serves 6.

French Potted Cheese in Wine

Grate 2 lbs. cheddar cheese on fine grater and combine with:

1 C. sour cream
1 t. chives, finely minced
1 t. salt
¼ t. mace
5 T. Sauterne Wine
½ C. melted butter

Mix well with a beater or whip in a blender. Pack into a 1-qt. buttered mold. Refrigerate overnight before using. Unmold on a serving tray with assorted crackers and fruits.

Greek

Greek Lemon-Rice Soup

Bring to a boil 2 qts. chicken stock (homemade or canned) and add 1 C. uncooked, regular rice. Cook until rice is tender—35 to 40 minutes. (Test!)

At high speed, beat 4 eggs until thick (about 5 minutes). Continue beating and add the juice of two lemons, a little at a time. Gradually, add 2 C. hot broth to the egg-lemon mixture, a little at a time. Now return the broth-egg-lemon mixture to the broth and rice in the kettle, hand stirring, constantly but gently. (A heavy yellow froth will remain on top of the soup in each serving portion!) Heat only to boiling point and serve immediately.

Serves 8.

Russian

Piroshki

These are a delicious meat and mushroom filled pastry which I like very much to make in miniature for appetizers. They can be made ahead and frozen, unbaked, when, and in the amount, needed.

Combine:
1 C. butter
1 8-oz. pkg. cream cheese, softened
¼ t. salt

Add:
2 C. sifted flour

Work together well with the fingertips and form into a ball. Wrap in waxed paper and chill overnight.

Next day, divide into four sections, working with one section at a time and keeping the rest chilled in the refrigerator until all is used. Roll out on a lightly floured board. Cut in 2-inch squares (for appetizers) or as large as you wish. Put about 1 heaping teaspoonful on square and fold in a triangle. Press with tines of a fork, along edges, to seal. Set seam sides up on an ungreased cookie sheet and bake at 350 degrees for 20 to 25 minutes or until only lightly brown.

Filling:
1 C. cooked meat (chicken, veal, or pork), finely minced
1 3-oz. can mushrooms, drained and minced
1 t. grated onion
1 hardboiled egg, minced fine
2 T. sour cream
1 t. flour
Dash nutmeg

½ t. dried dill weed
Dash paprika
Freshly ground pepper

Combine the above ingredients in a saucepan and heat until well blended, stirring constantly. Cool. Fill Piroshkis. Bake as directed above. Makes 2 to 2½ dozen appetizer-size pastries.

Stroganoff

(A delightful blend of beef and pork)

Remove the meat from 2 large pork chops and cube the meat. In a heavy skillet, melt 1 T. fat and add to it the pork cubes with 1 lb. beef chuck, cubed. Sprinkle lightly with ½ t. salt and a bit of fresh ground pepper. Brown slowly, stirring frequently. When brown, add 1 onion, chopped. Cook 2 minutes.

Add:
1 C. sliced celery
1 diced carrot
1 beef boullion cube (or ½ t. B.V.)

Stir in 1½ C. warm water. Cook slowly 30 minutes or until meat is fork tender. Combine 2 T. flour with ¼ C. warm water and stir into the pan with the meat and vegetables, adding 3 T. chili sauce, 2 T. worchestershire sauce, and a dash of tabasco. Stir until thickened and mixture boils. Reduce heat. Stir in 1 C. sour cream. (Taste to adjust need for salt.) Keep hot but do not boil.

In the meantime, cook an 8-oz. package of thin, short-length spaghetti, according to package directions. Serve meat and gravy over the drained spaghetti. Sprinkle with a small amount of Parmesan cheese.

Serves 4 or 5 generously.

East Indian

Many years ago, as I perused a mid-East cookbook, I came upon a saying which I believe has greatly influenced my attitude in cooking, for it echoed a thought I had often had, but couldn't find words for. "The food equals the affection," is the saying. It aptly sums up the spirit of hospitality and cooking—and of serving others. Think about it—it will make your labors much lighter!

Time and space do not allow me to give too many or too lengthy recipes for foreign cookery, but I hope you will try many of them and especially enjoy the East Indian recipes.

Indian Pilau

In 4 T. butter, saute 1 onion, minced, until limp but not brown. Add 1½ C. white regular rice and cook over low heat until lightly brown. Add 3 C. boiling chicken broth (homemade or canned), 1 clove garlic, pressed, 1 t. salt, and a few grinds of fresh pepper. Transfer all to a covered 2-qt. casserole. Cover and bake 30 minutes at 350 degrees. Remove cover and stir in ½ C. raisins which have been soaked in water to cover and drained. (This plumps up the raisins.) Replace cover and bake 15 minutes longer. Just before serving, garnish the top of the rice with ½ C. slivered almonds, lightly browned in 1 T. butter. Scatter a few finely sliced green onions over the top.

Serves 6.

Izmir Kufte

Combine:
1 lb. ground lean lamb (or beef)
1 egg
½ C. onion, finely minced
¼ C. parsley, very finely minced
1 C. soft bread crumbs
½ t. cummine
½ t. salt
⅛ t. pepper

Mix all ingredients well and form into thumb-shaped patties.

In a 400-degree oven, heat a baking pan with 3 T. butter. Put the little meat patties in the hot butter. With a pot holder covering your fingers, shake the pan so the patties become coated with the butter. Bake about 15 to 20 minutes, shaking the pan occasionally so they won't stick. Serve with Pilau.

Makes about 15 patties.

Classic Lamb Curry

In a heavy pan, brown 3 lbs. boneless, lean lamb (which has been cut in 1-inch cubes) in 2 T. butter. Remove meat from pan and, in the remaining fat, put 1 C. chopped onion, 1 clove garlic, pressed, 1 C. chopped, tart apple, and 1½ t. curry powder. Saute the vegetables until tender—about 5 minutes. Return the meat to the pan and stir well.

Add:
2 T. lemon juice
2 T. catsup
½ t. fresh grated ginger root (or ½ t. ground ginger)
1½ t. salt
1 bay leaf
1 small eggplant, peeled and diced
2 C. water

Bring to boiling point, reduce heat and simmer 1½ hours or until meat is very tender.

Mix 3 T. flour with ¼ C. water and stir into the pan juices. Stir until thickened. Add 1 T. brown sugar and ½ t. (more) curry powder. Keep warm preferably in a chafing dish. (This keeps very well at low temperature.) Serve white rice separately along with your choice of condiments (to be added according to *individual* taste!) Serve condiments in separate small dishes. Any of the following are a delightful accompaniment—use several:

Chopped green onions
Chopped green pepper
Whole salted peanuts
Flaked coconut
White or brown raisins
Sliced kumquats

Pineapple chunks

Yogurt (Homemade yogurt recipe is in the miscellaneous section of this book)

Serve your curry with "Chopatties" and a light dessert and you've got a marvelous meal, with very little effort.

Chapati
(An Indian Bread)

Sift together:

2 C. sifted flour

1 t. salt

Add:

¼ C. cooking oil

With the fingertips, work together until it resembles cornmeal. Stir in 8 T. water and ⅛ t. powdered cardamon (optional). Knead the dough until it looks satiny, about 7 or 8 minutes. Break off pieces of dough about 1½ inches in diameter and roll each into a 6-inch circle. Brown on both sides on a hot greased griddle. They will become bubbled and speckled with brown. Serve as bread with Classic Lamb Curry.

Makes 12 chapatis.

Chicken, India Style

Slowly simmer a 4-lb. chicken, left whole, in enough salted water to cover, until very tender. Remove from the kettle and remove skin and bones; cube the meat. In the meantime, simmer the broth until the stock is reduced to about 3 cups.

In a saucepan, combine 1 small (about 4-oz.) pkg. coconut with 1 C. milk. Bring to a boil; remove from heat and allow to stand for 25 minutes. Strain through a cheesecloth and reserve the coconut *milk,* but discard the coconut residue.

In a large, heavy pan, saute 1 C. chopped onion and 1 clove garlic, pressed, in 2 T. salad oil.

Add:
4 T. flour
½ t. saffron
½ t. ginger
½ t. dried red pepper flakes
½ t. salt

Stir in the reserved chicken broth, mixing thoroughly. Add the cubed chicken. Simmer gently about 10 minutes. Add the coconut milk. Serve over cooked noodles, rice, or bulgar wheat (cooked according to package directions).

Serves 6 to 8.

This dish may be served with condiments of your choice, listed with the recipe for Classic Lamb Curry.

Fruit Taj (A Simple Dessert)

Peel as many oranges as you need for a half orange to a serving. Section oranges, trimming away any tough membrane. Arrange orange sections in a sherbet dish with 2 whole, canned figs to each serving. Spoon over the fruit a sauce made of combining:

1 C. softened vanilla ice cream
1 beaten egg yolk
½ C. non-dairy whipped topping

Add:
1 T. rum or
1 T. rum flavoring, if desired

IRISH

Galantine of Fowl

Have your butcher bone (keep the bones for stock) a 4-lb. raw capon (or roasting chicken). Leave skin as whole as possible. Dip an old linen towel square, large enough to completely cover the fowl, in melted butter.

Place the fowl, skin side down on the cloth. Spread the skin open, discarding the skin from the back, and pat the meat firmly against the skin, leaving meat of legs to cover the filling. Make a forcement by mixing:

1 C. unseasoned, lean, ground pork with
1 C. smoked ground ham
1 egg
½ t. poultry seasons

Mix well and spread on the fowl; cover over with the meat from the leg and thighs and roll up in the cloth. Tie securely with string into a firm bundle. Place the bundle in a stew pan with 4 C. chicken broth (made from the bones and discarded skin), 2 carrots, unpeeled, 2 small onions, 2 sprigs parsley, and 6 whole peppercorns. Cover tightly. Simmer gently for 3 hours. Drain and cool. Remove cloth and chill overnight. Next day, prepare the glaze and decorate!

Over and Under Glaze

Under:
Soften 1 envelope unflavored gelatin in 3 T. cold water. Dissolve in 1 C. strained broth. When cool, add 1 T. salad dressing (such as Miracle Whip). Spoon over the fowl, several times, chilling after each addition. Decorate with parsley, olives, pimentos in an attractive pattern and return to refrigerator.

Over:
Add ½ envelope unflavored gelatin to 2 T. cold water. Dissolve in ½ C. hot water. Cool. Brush over the decorations and under glaze. Chill thoroughly. Serve on a cold platter with parsley trim. Slice with sharp knife when ready to serve.

POULTRY

For the money spent, there is little else that gives you as much value per dollar as poultry; be it chicken, turkey, ducklings, or game hens. Try some of these budget-wise recipes—you'll be glad you did!

Chicken Breasts Supreme

Sprinkle 3 large chicken breasts, cut in half lengthwise, with ½ t. salt and ½ t. paprika. (You may remove the skin, if you like.) Place in a baking dish.

Combine:
1 C. chicken broth (canned or bouillon)
¼ C. dry white wine
½ t. dried onion flakes
½ t. curry powder
Fresh ground black pepper

Pour the combination over the chicken breasts and cover (foil will do). Bake 1 hour. Uncover, bake 15 minutes more, or until meat is tender. Drain off juices from baking dish into a saucepan. Thicken with 2 T. flour mixed with ¼ C. warm water. Add 1 3-oz. can mushrooms and stir until thickened. Pour over the chicken breasts and serve with parsley—and pride!

Serves 6.

Leone's Turkey Terrapin

(Good using chicken, too!)

In a large saucepan, melt ½ C. butter; stir in ½ C. flour, ½ t. salt, and ⅛ t. pepper. Remove from heat and gradually stir in 3½ C. whole milk and 2 C. chicken broth. Return to heat and cook, stirring constantly, until thickened. Add and mix lightly:

2 C. canned or fresh, sliced mushrooms
4 hardcooked eggs, diced
1 No. 2 can green peas, drained
1 small jar pimientos
4 C. diced, cooked turkey

Heat thoroughly. At serving time, stir in 1 T. lemon juice.

Serves 8 to 10.

Serve on split "Southern Buttermilk Buscuits" (recipe included in this book under Breads Section), buttered.

Chicken Divan

This is a nice way to make leftovers "as good as most people's firsts!" Simple, too. Turkey may be substituted.

In a shallow baking dish, arrange 1 10-oz. pkg. frozen asparagus tips, cooked according to package directions, and drained well. Over the top, lay 6 or 8 slices of chicken breasts (or other chicken slices).

Blend 1 C. cream of chicken soup with 1/3 C. milk. Pour over chicken slices. Top with ½ C. shredded cheddar cheese. Bake at 450 degrees for 20 minutes, or until well heated and cheese is lightly brown.

Serves 4.

Adam's Casserole of Chicken

6 C. cornbread, crumbled
½ t. poultry seasoning
1 t. celery seed
⅛ t. pepper
½ t. salt
¼ C. minced onion
3 T. parsley, snipped
½ C. melted butter

Toss the above ingredients in a large bowl and spread evenly over the bottom of a buttered baking dish, 13 by 9 inches. Arrange 5 C. cooked chicken (canned, freshly cooked, or leftover) over the cornbread mixture.

In a saucepan, melt ¼ C. butter and add ¼ C. flour and 1 t. salt. Gradually add 2 C. chicken broth. Cook until thickened. Beat 2 eggs well, and add a little of the hot sauce to them, stirring well. Turn eggs into sauce and stir well. Stir in 3 C. milk and heat thoroughly. Turn over the cornbread and chicken. Bake at 375 degrees for 45 minutes, or until custard consistency is reached.

Serves 8 to 10.

Cornish Hens with Pecan-Fruit Stuffing

Wash, clean, and pat dry with paper toweling, 4 rock Cornish game hens. Place breast side up in a small roaster.

In a large saucepan, melt 4 T. butter and, in it, saute ¼ C. sliced green onions. Add 1 3-oz. can mushroom pieces and cook gently for 5 minutes. Add ½ C. pecans, chopped, ¼ C. white raisins, 1 C. diced tart apple, and 2 C. diced day-old bread. Sprinkle over all ½ t. salt and ½ t. sugar. Mix well and stuff the hens with the mixture. Close the cavity with a skewer in each. Bake at 350 degrees for 1 to 1½ hours (depending on the size of the hens) or until very tender. Baste every 15 minutes with a mixture of ¼ C. melted butter and ¼ C. water. Serve, sprinkled with chopped parsley and a garnish of mandarin oranges, if desired.

Serves 4 generously!

Turkey Paprika

(A fine chafing dish entree)

In ¼ C. butter, saute 1 C. diced onion and 1 small clove garlic, pressed, until tender but not brown. Add 1 10-oz. can tomato sauce with mushrooms, 1 t. paprika, ½ t. salt, ⅛ t. pepper, and 1 T. lemon juice, 1 C. chicken broth (canned is fine), and 3 C. leftover diced turkey. Simmer slowly for about 20 minutes. Transfer to a hot chafing dish and stir in 1 C. sour cream. Heat thoroughly over the hot water in the bottom of the chafing dish. Serve on cooked noodles that have been tossed with a little butter and 1 t. poppy seeds.

Serves 4.

Sesame Fried Chicken

Quarter two 3-lb. broiling chickens.

Combine:
4 T. sesame seeds
1 C. flour
½ t. poultry seasoning
½ t. paprika
⅛ t. pepper
½ t. salt

In a bowl, put 2/3 C. undiluted, evaporated milk and dip each chicken quarter in it. Dip chicken into sesame seed and flour mixture.

Heat ½ C. butter and ¼ C. salad oil in a heavy skillet (or two skillets, if they seem crowded). Saute chicken quarters, over low heat, until golden brown and tender, turning frequently. Caution: Do *not* have heat too high, as sesame seeds brown rapidly—you want them just golden!

Serves 6.

Chicken or Turkey Souffle

(If you have the cooked chicken or turkey—most likely you have everything else on the cupboard shelf!)

Combine:
2 C. cooked chicken or turkey
¼ C. diced onion
¼ C. diced green pepper
½ C. chopped celery
¾ t. salt
¼ t. pepper

Cube 6 slices of white bread and place half of it in the bottom of a 2-qt. casserole. Cover with the chicken (or turkey) and vegetables mixture. Top with remaining bread cubes.

Combine 2 beaten eggs and 1½ C. whole milk and pour over all. Do *not* stir. Refrigerate overnight.

At cooking time, combine ½ C. mayonnaise and 1 8-oz. can mushroom soup and spread over top of mixture in the casserole. Bake at 325 degrees for 1 hour. Sprinkle with ½ C. shredded, processed cheddar cheese and return to oven until cheese melts, about 10 minutes. Do not stir!

Serves 8.

I want to include a duckling recipe in this section, but I find that the most wonderful recipe I have is found in the Oriental Section of the Foreign Cookery Chapter. It is "Purple Plum Duckling." Try it!

FROSTINGS

Often the recipe for frosting is included with the cake recipe, but here are a few unusually good ones you will enjoy.

Sour Cream Velvet

Melt 1 6-oz. pkg. semi-sweet chocolate bits over hot water with ¼ C. butter. Remove from heat and add:

½ C. sour cream
1 t. vanilla
Dash of salt

Gradually beat in 2½ to 2¾ C. sifted, powdered sugar. This is enough to frost a 2 (9-inch) layer cake or a 10-inch angel cake.

"Old Stand-By" Struesel Topping

Mix together:
½ C. light brown sugar
2 T. flour
2 t. cinnamon
2 T. melted butter
¼ C. finely cut pecans

Spread on a freshly baked, warm cake. Return cake to oven for 5 to 7 minutes. Especially good on applesauce cake.

Chocolate Pudding Frosting

Cook 1 4-oz. pkg. of chocolate pudding according to package directions using only 1½ C. milk. Cover surface with wax paper and cool.

Cream ½ C. butter or margarine and ¼ C. vegetable shortening with 1 C. sifted powdered sugar, until fluffy. Stir in 1 t. vanilla and ¼ t. salt. Gradually beat in the chocolate pudding. Makes enough to frost top and sides of a 2 layer 9-inch cake.

Creamy Lemon Frosting

Whip together:

½ C. soft butter

1 egg

¼ t. salt

with an electric mixer. Stir in 3 C. sifted, powdered sugar, ¼ C. light corn syrup, and 3 T. lemon juice plus the grated rind of 1 lemon. Beat all together and add 2 drops yellow food color. Makes enough to frost 3 dozen cupcakes or 1 large 10-inch angel or chiffon cake.

Mama's 7-Minute Frosting

In the top of a double boiler, over simmering water, combine 2 eggwhites, unbeaten, 1½ C. sugar, 5 T. water, and 1½ t. light corn syrup. Beat with an electric mixer (or rotary beater) for 7 minutes or until the frosting stands in stiff peaks. Remove from heat; beat in 1 t. vanilla. Continue beating until frosting is glossy and holds its place.

Mama used to frost a chocolate layer cake with this and then dribble *melted bitter chocolate* over all so that it ran down, in ribbons, along the sides. Beautiful and yummy!

MEAT

Like most cooks, I plan the rest of my meal around the choice of meat. We all know certain things are almost traditional "go-togethers"—like ham and sweet potatoes and corned beef and cabbage. However, I think to depart from the beaten path and try something new and different adds zest to what might otherwise be an ordinary meal. Here are a few favorites—simple and delicious.

Mom Hoegh's Ham Loaf

Have your butcher grind together:

¾ lb. smoked ham
2 lbs. lean pork shoulder

To the ground meat, add:

1½ C. milk
1 C. soft bread crumbs
2 eggs, beaten
¾ t. salt
⅛ t. pepper
1 medium onion, finely diced
1 T. green pepper, finely diced

Mix well. Form in a shallow baking dish. Bake 1 hour and 15 minutes at 350 degrees. During the last 15 minutes the loaf may be glazed with 2 T. chili sauce *or* a glaze made by boiling together for 3 minutes:

½ C. brown sugar
3 T. vinegar
2 t. dry mustard

Baste the loaf every 10 minutes for the last half hour of baking time.

Serves 10. Serve with Noodles Romanoff!

Savory Meatballs

These are excellent for use in Italian spaghetti sauce, creamed, or with any sauce you prefer.

Combine:
1 lb. lean hamburger
1 egg, slightly beaten
½ onion, minced fine
1 t. dry mustard
1 t. salt
¼ t. pepper
¼ t. poultry seasoning
¼ C. yellow cornmeal
½ C. milk

Mix well and shape into 16 balls. Roll balls lightly in flour and brown in 2 T. fat. Cook gently 15 to 20 minutes in sauce of your choice.

Broiled Ham with Honey Sauce

Simple and so delicious!

Broil a full cut of ready-to-eat ham slice, 1½ inches thick, on an outdoor grill or in the broiler, 5 minutes to a side, basting *often* with the following sauce:

Shred the rind from 2 oranges, pound with a pestil (or smash with a spatula handle), mix with ½ C. honey, 2 T. vinegar, and ¼ t. liquid smoke (Wright's). Put in a jar, cover, and shake well. Serves 6. Try my recipe for Scalloped Potatoes with this and fresh asparagus with brown-buttered almonds on top! Scrumptious!

Gourmet Veal Loaf

In a large bowl combine:

1½ lbs. ground raw veal
2 C. grated raw carrots
¼ C. onion, chopped fine
1 3-oz. can mushroom pieces, chopped
½ C. fine soft bread crumbs
1 t. salt
¼ t. pepper
1 C. sour cream

Mix lightly with a fork. Mold into a loaf by packing into a 9 x 5 x 3 inch loaf pan. Invert onto a shallow pan and carefully remove the loaf pan. Bake at 375 degrees for 1 hour or until golden brown on top.

Place the loaf on a heatproof platter and edge with fluffy mashed potatoes on each side and tomato halves on the ends. Brush the vegetables with melted butter and parsley. Broil all for 10 minutes or until potatoes brown a little!

Serves 6 generously.

Hamburger Loaf (Different!)

Combine in a large bowl:
1½ lbs. hamburger
1 can vegetarian vegetable soup, undiluted
½ C. water
1 C. uncooked, quick-cooking oatmeal
½ t. sage, rubbed fine
1¼ t. salt
⅛ t. pepper
¼ C. onion, finely minced
1 T. celery leaves, minced
1 T. green pepper, minced
1 egg, unbeaten

Mix well and shape into a loaf in a shallow pan. Bake at 350 degrees for 1 hour and 15 minutes. Baste frequently with the pan juices.

Serves 6.

Beef-Mushroom "Steak"

Economical and delish!

Combine:
1 lb. hamburger
¾ C. soft white bread crumbs
½ can cream of mushroom soup
¾ t. salt
⅛ t. pepper
1 egg, unbeaten
1 T. green pepper, minced fine
1 T. green onion, minced fine

In a 9-inch skillet, melt 2 T. fat and pat the steak into it. (It should be about ½ inch thick.) Bake 25 minutes at 325 degrees. Put under the broiler for 5 minutes more to brown the top well. Serves 4 generously! Use the remaining soup for a sauce by mixing the ½ can of soup with 3 T. milk or cream. Serve meat in wedges with the sauce on top.

Herburger Pie

Here is a meal in one dish!

Make an 8-inch pastry crust from your own favorite recipe (or a packaged mix may be used). Bake as usual. While crust is baking, brown 1 lb. lean ground beef in 2 T. butter and add ½ t. salt, ⅛ t. *each* of pepper, garlic, salt, thyme, marjoram, and nutmeg. Add 1 T. minced onion, 1 T. minced parsley, 1 T. lemon juice. Blend in 1 can frozen cream of potato soup, which has been defrosted. Heat thoroughly and spoon into the baked pastry shell. Top with ½ C. grated cheddar cheese, and bake 10 minutes.

Makes 4 generous servings. All you need to complete the meal is a tossed green salad, hot rolls, and a simple fruit dessert, such as "Pineapple Simplicity."

Veal Superb

Have 2 lbs. veal steak cut ¾ inch thick. Cut into serving pieces and dip each piece in a mixture of 1 beaten egg and 2 T. cream. Dip into cracker crumbs and brown slowly in 4 T. butter (more, if needed). When golden brown, transfer meat to a shallow 9- x 13-inch baking dish.

Combine:

1 can cream of chicken soup, undiluted
½ C. sour cream
¼ C. stuffed,green olives, sliced
½ t. marjoram

Pour the sauce over the veal steaks and bake at 350 degrees for 1 hour, or until fork-tender.

Serves 8. (Serve with small, new potatoes in a cream sauce with fresh or frozen green peas, tomato and cucumber salad, and "Lemon Dainty" for a really superb meal!)

Barbecued Hamburgers A La Leone

A make-ahead—so easy!

Combine:
2 lbs. hamburger
½ C. soft bread crumbs
1 t. salt
⅛ t. pepper
2 T. grated onion
½ C. milk

Make into 12 patties (bun size) and saute lightly, a few at a time, in 2 t. fat.

In the meantime, dice ½ lb. bacon and fry until crisp. Drain off fat and reserve the bacon. In the same pan, saute 1 C. onion, cut fine (in 1 T. fat) with 1 green pepper, diced fine, and 1 C. celery, diced fine.

Add:
1 10-oz. bottle catsup
1 can tomato soup
1 soup can of water

Cook all together, slowly, for 30 minutes. Add 1 4-oz. can mushrooms and stir well. Place the cooked hamburgers in the sauce and allow to stand until serving time. Reheat and serve.

Makes 12 servings.

Swiss Ham A La King

Melt 3 T. butter in a large saucepan and add 3 T. flour; stir until smooth. Remove from heat and add 2½ C. milk, ¼ t. salt. Stir well and return to medium heat, stirring constantly until slightly thickened. Add 2½ C. cooked ham, cut in cubes (fat discarded), 1 C. grated Swiss cheese, ½ t. worchestershire sauce, and a dash of tabasco sauce. Stir until cheese is melted and sauce is smooth. Add 1 T. sweet pickle relish and 2 T. chopped pimiento. Serve on toasted English muffins, buttered.

Serves 6.

Braised Beef in Claret Sauce With Vegetables

Make a marinade by combining:

½ C. claret wine
2 T. lemon juice
¼ C. onion, finely chopped
2 T. parsley, minced
1 bay leaf
2 whole cloves
1½ t. salt
¼ t. pepper
¼ t. paprika
⅛ t. thyme

Cut in 1-inch cubes, 3 lbs. top round steak. Pour marinade over meat and allow to stand 4 or 5 hours. Remove meat and drain well. (Reserve marinade.) In a large heavy kettle, melt 3 T. fat; add meat and brown slowly on all sides. Add 1 No. 2 can small boiling onions, drained, and 10 to 15 fresh mushrooms (washed and trimmed). Toss lightly until mushrooms are lightly browned. Remove meat, onions, and mushrooms from pan and stir into the fat that remains in the pan 3 T. flour. Stir well, scraping the bits of brown from the bottom of the pan. Add 4 C. beef boullion and stir until lightly thickened.

Return the meat only to the gravy and cook, covered, on low heat for 2½ to 3 hours, or until meat is tender. One-half hour before serving time, add the reserved vegetables and 3 carrots, cut in ½-inch pieces. Cook until carrots are tender. Spoon the meat into the center of a hot platter and surround with the vegetables. Strain the gravy and pour over all.

Serves 6 to 8. Serve with rice, a tossed salad, onion rolls, and a simple fruit dessert.

Standing Prime Rib Roast

In choosing a rib roast, one should buy at least four pounds or more, as it is difficult to cook a smaller piece to a perfect degree of doneness. Also, if you don't already have one, *do* invest in a meat thermometer—it's the only way to be sure of perfect results. Allow at least ½ lb. per serving.

Place meat fat side up in a shallow roasting pan. Do not cover. (Gash the fat in several places and insert slivers of fresh garlic cloves in each, if desired.)

The fat will baste the meat as it cooks and the ribs will keep the meat off the bottom of the pan. Insert the meat thermometer into the thick part of the meat and do not allow it to touch any bone. Roast meat at 325 degrees. Do not add water!

Weight	**Doneness**	**Time**	**Thermometer Temperature**
4 lbs.	Rare	1½ hours	140 degrees F.
	Medium	2 hrs.	160 degrees F.
	Well	2 hrs. 20 min.	170 degrees F.
6 lbs.	Rare	2 hrs.	140 degrees F.
	Medium	2½ hrs.	160 degrees F.
	Well	3 hrs. 20 min.	170 degrees F.
8 lbs.	Rare	2 hrs. 50 min.	140 degrees F.
	Medium	3 hrs. 20 min.	160 degrees F.
	Well	4 hrs. 20 min.	170 degrees F.

Chicken Fried Liver

Sprinkle 1½ lbs. sliced liver with 3 T. lemon juice. Let stand 5 minutes. Combine ¼ C. flour, 1 t. salt, ¼ t. pepper and dip each slice of liver in it.

In a separate bowl, combine ¼ C. milk, 2 T. grated onion, 1 beaten egg. Dip the floured liver sliced into the milk mixture and then into finely crushed cracker crumbs (about 1½ C.).

Heat ½ C. salad oil and 1 T. butter in a heavy frying pan. Saute the liver slices over medium heat about 4 minutes per side. Serve with onion rings, if desired.

Serves 6.

Swiss Steak

Combine ¼ C. flour, ½ t. salt, ⅛ t. pepper. Cut 2 lbs. thick top round of beef into serving pieces. Dredge beef in flour mixture and pound well with a meat mallet (to force the flour into the tissue). In a heavy skillet melt 2 T. bacon fat (or oil) and brown the meat well, on both sides, over medium heat. Push meat aside and add ½ C. chopped onion to the pan. Saute a few minutes until onion is lightly brown. Mix the following ingredients and pour over the meat in the skillet:

1 10-oz. can onion soup, undiluted
1/3 C. water
1 T. prepared mustard
2 T. tomato paste
1 T. worchestershire sauce

Cover skillet and simmer slowly for 2 to 2½ hours or until very tender. Remove meat to a warm platter and thicken the gravy with flour mixed to a thin paste with a small amount of water.

Serves 6. The steak, served with parsleyed new (or small) boiled potatoes, is ideal.

Veal Birds

Cut 1½ lbs. veal steak into 3- x 5-inch pieces. Spread with Savory Dressing: 3 C. small-diced toasted bread cubes.

Combine:

½ C. milk
1 egg, beaten
2 T. minced parsley
2 T. minced onion
2 T. minced celery
½ t. salt
¼ t. pepper

Mix well and chill. Spread on veal steaks and roll up, jelly-roll fashion. Tie with string or secure with toothpicks. Brown rolls in 3 T. fat. Transfer to a 2-qt. baking dish. Heat 1 C. chicken broth (canned or homemade) in the pan (in which you have browned the meat), and pour over the veal birds. Bake at 350 degrees for 1½ hours.

Serves 4 to 6. It is a pretty platter when the birds are surrounded, alternately, with French style green beans, and julienne-sliced carrots. Tuck a bit of parsley in at the ends!

You will find many more meat recipes by consulting the chapter on "Outdoor Cooking" in this book.

MISC.

Yogurt

In a quart jar, shake together 2 C. water and 1½ C. powdered skim dry milk until well mixed. Add more water to fill the quart jar. Pour into a large mixing bowl. Add 4 T. commercial yogurt (plain) and 1 10½-oz. can undiluted evaporated milk (such as Pet Milk) and 1 C. lukewarm water. Pour into 4 or 5 pint-size jars and put in a large covered pan (such as a preserving kettle). Cover within 2 inches of top of jars with *lukewarm* (not hot) water.

Set the kettle into your electric skillet—set temperature control on warm (just barely above OFF indication). Allow to remain in this warm water bath for 3 to 5 hours. Test occasionally, *after two hours,* by moving one of the jars slightly to see if it has coagulated to consistency of custard.

When you think the yogurt is ready, take some up on a teaspoon; it should hold its shape.

Caution: Do not let water in pan become too warm or your yogurt will separate! (If it separates, it can still be used in pancakes; in fact, it's very good!) After making it once, your own yogurt may be used for a starter.

Marrow Dumplings With Chives

Use the dumplings in homemade beef or chicken stock. In fact, these are very good in a big pot of homemade vegetable soup where the marrow of the bone is readily available. Crack beef shin bones, or have your butcher do it—dig out the marrow with a narrow blade knife.

To 2 T. mashed marrow, add 3 T. sifted bread crumbs, ½ t. minced chives, ⅛ t. salt, and a dash of pepper. Moisten mixture with enough egg white so it may be made into small balls. Drop dumplings into boiling stock and cook 5 minutes or until they rise to the surface. Serve immediately.

Makes 6 to 8 balls. Recipe may be doubled or tripled.

Old Fashioned Venison Mincemeat

A fine addition to your winter freezer supply. In a large preserving kettle, combine:

2 lbs. (4 to 4½ C.) ground, cooked venison
1½ lbs. beef suet, ground
2 qts. tart apples, peeled and diced fine
2 C. sugar
½ C. molasses
1 qt. apple cider
1 lb. currants
2 lbs. seedless raisins
1 C. meat stock (or canned broth)

Mix well together and cook, covered, for 2 hrs. at low temperature. Stir occasionally.

Add:
2 C. grape juice
1 C. brown sugar
1 t. cinnamon
1 t. nutmeg
½ t. allspice
1½ t. salt
1 4-oz. pkg. candied pineapple, slivered
1 4-oz. pkg. candied citron, minced.

Bring to a boil again, reduce heat, and simmer for 1 hour longer or until the mincemeat is thickened. Cool. Pack into 1-qt. freezer containers. Freeze. Yields about 5 qts. (Use 1 qt. to a pie or combine with apples enough to make 2 8-inch pies. We like it, as is!)

Glaze for Fruit Pies

In a small saucepan, blend together 1 T. cornstarch, a dash of salt, and ½ C. fruit juice (cherry, strawberry, grape—or your choice). Add 2 drops of (blending) food color and 1/3 C. white corn syrup. Cook over low heat, stirring constantly until mixture thickens. Remove from heat, cover, and cool. Arrange fruit over pie (or cake) and pour the glaze over it, evenly as possible. Chill. Serve with whipped cream, if desired. (This is beautiful on a strawberry chiffon pie!)

Kumquat Flowers

A decorative touch for an Oriental dinner or pretty on a glazed ham.

Cut each kumquat, halfway through, twice—to form four petals. With a sharp knife, roll back the petals and press a candied or maraschino cherry into the center. Impale on a toothpick for easy anchoring to the meat.

Quick Peach Pickles

Delicious, and they keep their color.

Drain a No. 2½ can peach halves (I use a firm kind, such as Del Monte or Kuner [a Colorado packer]). Put the syrup into a 2-qt. saucepan with ¾ C. brown sugar (packed firm), ½ C. vinegar, 2 sticks cinnamon, 1 t. whole cloves, and 1 t. whole allspice. Bring to a boil; reduce heat and simmer 5 minutes. Add peach halves and simmer 5 minutes. Spoon the peaches, carefully, into a wide-mouth quart jar (or a bowl) and pour the hot syrup over. Allow to stand, refrigerated, overnight, before using. Serve chilled.

Apricot Cornflake Toast

Combine:
2 eggs
½ C. apricot nectar
¼ t. salt

Beat well. Dip 8 slices firm-textured white bread into the mixture and then into 2 C. crushed cornflakes. Pan fry in 3 to 4 T. butter, turning once, and adding a bit more butter, if necessary. Serve hot with syrup, jelly, or sifted, powdered sugar.

Makes 4 servings.

Mr. Hite's Scrapple

Cook 2½ lbs. very lean pork shoulder until very tender. Remove meat from bone, reserve broth, and grind the meat. Measure the broth and add enough water to make 3 quarts, into a deep kettle. Add the meat, 1½ t. salt, 1 t. pepper, and 1 T. poultry seasoning. Stir in 2 2/3 C. yellow cornmeal. (By adding the cornmeal before the mixture comes to a boil, it prevents lumping!) Stir the mixture constantly until it comes to a boil. Cover and simmer *slowly* for 2 to 3 hours or until very thick. Stir frequently with a long-handled spoon. Oil two loaf tins 9 x 4 x 3 inches, and pour the mixture into mold. Chill. At serving time, slice in ½-inch thick slices; dredge with flour and fry in hot fat until well browned and hot.

Makes about 15 or 16 slices—you should have at least two slices per serving. Serve with syrup and butter-basted eggs.

Butter-Basted Eggs

Over *low* heat, melt 2 T. butter in a skillet. Add the desired number of eggs and sprinkle with 1 T. water. Cover closely. Cook to the desired degree of doneness without turning, from 3 to 6 minutes.

Hot Stuffed Avocados

Wash gently 3 ripe avocados and cut each in two, lengthwise. Remove seeds and sprinkle a little lemon juice over them. Place halves in a shallow baking dish and prepare the following filling:

Combine:
1 1-lb. can red salmon, skin and bones removed
½ C. mayonnaise
2 T. lemon juice
1 t. chili sauce
¼ t. powdered garlic
½ t. worchestershire sauce

Mix well and divide evenly among the six avocado halves. Bake at 350 degrees for 20 to 25 minutes. Top each half with a dollop of sour cream (about ½ C. in all) and sprinkle lightly with paprika. Very nice meal served with Oven-Fried Potatoes.

Oven-Fried Potatoes

Parboil in salted water to cover 6 small potatoes or 6 halves of larger potatoes, for 20 minutes. In a glass baking dish, melt 4 T. butter; turn the drained potatoes into it and sprinkle lightly with salt, pepper, and paprika. Bake at 350 degrees for 30 to 35 minutes, shaking the dish frequently so potatoes brown evenly.

Serves 6. Don't forget the parsley and a pickled peach!

Sour (Cream) Grapes

Wash and slice in two 1½ lbs. seedless green grapes (about 3 C.). In a shallow bowl, combine ¾ C. sour cream and ½ C. light brown sugar, packed, and *then* sifted. Add the grapes and toss lightly, mixing well. Chill about 2 hours. Spoon into pretty serving dishes and put a teaspoon of sour cream on top of each serving. Dust with a bit of sifted brown sugar (simple and delish!)

Shelling Brazil nuts is simple if they're frozen. Shells are brittle—shatter easily, nuts come out whole. Do only a few at a time, keeping remainder frozen as you work.

Yes—I believe you'd class this under miscellaneous! I've saved this recipe many years!

Husband Conserve

Select the best man you can find and brush him carefully to rid him of indifference. Be careful not to beat him as you would an egg or cream, for beating will make him tough and apt to froth at the mouth.

Lift him gently into the home-preserving kettle and tie him with strong cords of affection which are not easily broken. Do not sear him with sarcasm, for that causes spitting and sputtering which may ultimately result in spontaneous combustion. Scramble when difficulty arises.

Do not soak him in liquor either, for excessive draughts will make him mushy and spongy with your friends, and in Colorado stewed husbands are not too popular.

It is best to let him simmer tenderly at will, to blend tactfully with dressing and seasoning. Stuff him one hour before taking out or before asking a great favor of him. A little caress or a glass of water will often add tenderness.

Flavor him with oil of happiness, an ounce of understanding, and a bushel of laughter and fun.

Need him; need his dough, and be sure to save some of the dough for the little dumplings.

—Author Unknown

PICKLES & PRESERVING

Here are a few recipes for that special "extra" touch so welcome when you're looking for something different. Several of the recipes in this chapter can be made in quantity to keep on your shelf and can be added to a simple meal, at a moment's notice!

Mama's Bread and Butter Pickles

Select 4- or 5-inch cucumbers. Wash and dry. Cut in thin slices without removing the rind.

1 qt. sliced cucumbers
6 small onions, thinly sliced

Sprinkle the cucumbers and onions with 3 T. salt. Let stand one hour. Drain in a collander, pressing with the fingertips.

In a large kettle, put:

1½ C. vinegar
2¼ C. sugar
1 t. celery seed
1 t. tumeric powder
½ t. cinnamon
2 green peppers, diced

Bring to a boil and add the cucumber and onion slices. Boil together, over medium heat, for 20 minutes. Bottle while hot and seal.

Makes 3 pints.

Virginia Chunk Pickles

Don't let the length of this recipe scare you. The end result is well worth every minute of the effort. This is the best pickle I have ever eaten—always crisp and sweet-spicy!

Take 60 medium size cucumbers (they must be solid, green, and not developed so much that the seeds are large). Cut them in chunks and place in a stone crock or enameled kettle. You should have about 2 gallons of chunks.

Heat brine solution, using 2 C. salt to one gallon water. Pour, boiling hot, over cucumber chunks. Let stand in a cool place *one week*. Drain. If need be, skim top. On the 8th, 9th, and 10th days, pour (a fresh solution every day—drain and discard solution each day) over chunks, an alum bath (using 1 gallon boiling water and 1 T. powdered alum). At the end of this period, drain. Make a pickling solution of 6 C. vinegar, 5 C. sugar, ½ C. mixed pickling spices, and 1 T. celery seed. Bring to a boil and pour over the pickle chunks. Allow to stand four days. On the 5th day, pour off the solution into a large pan; add 2 C. sugar. Bring to a boil and pour over chunks. On 6th morning, drain into pan again, and add 1 C. sugar. Bring to a boil. Pack the pickle chunks into sterilized jars and pour the hot syrup over them, filling jars within ½ inch of the top. Seal as usual.

Makes 14 to 16 pints.

Colorado Relish

A fine way to use the tomatoes, at the end of the season, that might get caught in the frost—especially in Colorado's short growing season.

Chop together until very fine the following ingredients:

3 pts. green tomatoes (6 C.)
3 pts. ripe tomatoes (6 C.)
1 medium head cabbage
1 qt. onions, cut up (to measure)
2 medium bunches celery

Add ¼ C. salt to the above and mix well. Let mixture stand overnight. In the morning, drain. Put in a large preserving kettle and add:

3 pts. cider vinegar
3 pts. sugar
½ t. cinnamon
½ t. cloves
¼ C. mustard seed
1 2-oz. bottle horseradish

Cook all together, over medium heat, stirring frequently, about 30 minutes or until thickened. Pour into sterilized jars and seal.

Makes 6 pints.

Golden Relish

Clean and chop (not too fine):

4 C. carrots, cut up (to measure)
4 C. celery, cut up
2 green peppers
2 pimientos

Add:
4 tart apples, peeled and chopped
2 C. sugar
2 C. cider vinegar
2 T. salt
2 T. celery seed

Cook gently in a large preserving kettle until the vegetables are tender and the mixture has slightly thickened—about 30 to 40 minutes.

Makes about 6 pints.

Mom Hoegh's Peach Marmalade

Wash, quarter, and remove seeds from 1 lemon and 2 oranges. Press out most of juice into a 1½-qt. saucepan. With a very sharp knife, slice the rinds very thin. Put the sliced rinds into the juice. Cover and cook over low heat until rinds are tender, stirring frequently. (Do not allow to scorch!) When tender, turn into a large preserving kettle and add:

3 C. Colorado peaches, sliced thin

Cook until peaches are tender and clear. Add 1 C. crushed pineapple with juice and 5 C. sugar. Bring to a rolling boil. Cook until a jellied surface forms on a cold testing plate. Remove from heat and add a few sliced maraschino cherries (red and green are especially nice if you want to use this at Christmastime for gifts. Unusual and delicious!) Seal jars with parafin.

Makes 7 or 8 1-C. jars.

Pear Honey

Unusual and marvelous on Sour Dough Pancakes.

4 C. crushed ripe pears
1 C. crushed pineapple
8 C. sugar

Combine ingredients in a large preserving kettle and bring to a full rolling boil. Boil 1 minute. Remove from heat and add ½ bottle Certo. Stir and cool slightly. Pour into sterilized jars and seal.

Makes 8 to 10 ½-C. jars.

Strawberry Jam For The Freezer

Just like eating fresh berries!

Mix 4 C. crushed strawberries and 5 C. sugar and allow to stand 10 minutes. In a 2-qt. saucepan, quickly mix 1 C. water and 1 pkg. powdered pectin (such as M.C.P.). Bring to a boil and boil 1 minute, stirring constantly to dissolve. Add the berries and sugar mixture and stir well.

Remove from heat (berries should not cook at all!). Pour into sterilized jars and cool until set. Jam may be frozen, but will keep in the refrigerator a month.

Makes 4 or 5 1-C. jars.

Unique Rhubarb Jam

Clean and finely dice 4 C. rhubarb and combine with 4 C. sugar in a large bowl. Let stand overnight. In the morning, put in a large preserving kettle. Bring to a rolling boil and cook 5 minutes. Remove from heat and stir in 1 pkg. raspberry gelatin. Put in clean jars to set. Refrigerate.

Makes 5 or 6 1-C. jars. Keep refrigerated! Do not freeze.

Mom's Blueberry-Rhubarb Jam

An original recipe—use canned blueberries

Drain the juice from 2 No. 2 cans blueberries into a large preserving kettle and reserve the berries. To the juice, add 4 C. small-size, diced pink rhubarb. Cook 5 minutes.

Add the blueberries and 1/3 C. lemon juice. (You should have 4½ C. fruit and juice—add water to mixture to make this amount, if needed.) Add 1 pkg. powdered pectin (such as M.C.P. or Sure-Jell). Bring to a full boil; gradually stir in 5½ C. sugar. Boil 1 minute. Remove from heat and stir several minutes. Pour into sterilized jars and seal.

Makes about 6 to 8 1-C. jars.

Colorado Peachy-Plum Jam

Finely chop enough ripe peaches to make 2½ C. fruit. Sprinkle with ¼ C. lemon juice.

In a large saucepan, combine 2 C. diced, ripe, unpeeled red plums (the tart Red Goose plum is ideal), with ¼ C. water and simmer 5 minutes. Add the prepared peaches and lemon juice, along with ½ t. butter and 7½ C. sugar. Bring the total mixture to a full rolling boil and boil rapidly for 1 minute, stirring constantly. Remove from heat and add ½ bottle Certo. Stir several minutes to prevent fruit from floating. Pour into sterilized jars and seal.

Makes 8 1-C. jars of *the best jam*!

PIES & CRUSTS

Pie—the masterpiece of desserts, full of fruit, or light as air, soft, crunchy—all delicious! Serve any of the following recipes and earn your crown. My mother was an expert in pie making and many of her recipes are included.

Mama's Green Tomato Pie

An old-fashioned favorite!

Prepare a 2-crust pastry according to your favorite recipe or use mine at the *end* of this chapter.

Slice 5 or 6 firm, green tomatoes of medium size into a bowl, slicing them about ⅛ inch thick. Cover with boiling water. Let stand 5 minutes and drain.

Mix well:
1 C. sugar
¼ t. salt
2½ T. flour
¼ t. nutmeg
A pinch of cloves
Juice and grated rind of 1 lemon

Add the sugar mixture to the sliced tomatoes and toss lightly.

Put the mixture into a 9-inch pastry-lined pie plate and dot with 4 T. butter. Cover with the top crust; seal edges by fluting with your fingertips. Prick top with a sharp-tined fork and sprinkle with a mixture of 2 t. sugar and ¼ t. cinnamon.

Bake at 450 degrees for 10 minutes (set timer!). Reduce heat and continue baking at 325 degrees for 40 minutes. Cool slightly. Serve with a thin wedge of sharp cheddar cheese or vanilla ice cream. You'll have a pleasant surprise in store for you!

Mabel's Cloud Pie

Separate 4 eggs. Beat whites until frothy and *very gradually* add 1½ C. sugar mixed with ¼ t. cream of tartar. Beat until the mixture forms peaks. Butter a 9-inch pie plate, and turn the egg white (meringue) mixture into the pan and form a shell, higher at the edges. Bake at 275 degrees for 1 hour. Cool.

Beat the 4 remaining egg yolks with ½ C. sugar until lemon colored. Add 1 drop yellow food color and 3 T. lemon juice and 1 T. grated lemon rind. Cook in the top of a double boiler, over simmering water, until thickened. Cool, covered!

Whip ½ pint whipping cream until it holds soft peaks. Fold into the cooled lemon-egg yolk mixture. Fill the meringue shell. Chill 2 or 3 hours.

Serves 6 generously—or 8 average-size portions.

Mama's Best Pumpkin Pie

Make a pastry shell for a 9-inch single crust pie. (Use your own favorite recipe or mine, at the end of this chapter.)

Combine:
2 eggs, beaten
¾ C. brown sugar
1½ C. cooked pumpkin
¼ t. ginger
1 t. cinnamon
½ t. salt
1 C. milk
½ C. cream (or Half & Half)

Turn the filling into the crust and bake at 450 degrees for 15 minutes. Reduce heat to 325 degrees for 30 minutes more. Serve with or without whipped cream or soft ice cream.

6 average portions.

Variation: On the bottom of the unbaked crust, spread a mixture of 1/3 C. brown sugar, 1/3 C. pecans, chopped, and 1 T. cold butter. Mix the last three ingredients by crumbling together with your fingertips. Gently pour in the pumpkin mixture so as not to disturb the "Praline" mix! Very rich—no cream, please.

Pumpkin Chiffon Pie

Mix well and pat into a 9-inch pie plate:

1½ C. crushed gingersnaps
1/3 C. powdered sugar
½ C. melted butter

For the filling: In the top of a double boiler, combine:
3 egg yolks, beaten
½ C. sugar
1¼ C. pumpkin
½ C. milk
½ t. ginger
½ t. cinnamon
½ t. nutmeg
½ t. salt

Cook over simmering water until thick. To the hot mixture, add 1 envelope of plain gelatin which has been softened in ¼ C. water. Cool. When cool and thickened, beat (until they hold soft peaks) the 3 remaining egg whites with ½ C. sugar. Fold gently into the pumpkin-gelatin mixture until thoroughly mixed. Pour into the gingersnap crust. Chill. Top with whipped cream, if desired.

Rhubarb Chiffon Pie

Dissolve 1 pkg. of lemon gelatin and 1/3 C. sugar in ¾ C. *boiling* water (stir thoroughly until all is dissolved). Add 1 T. lemon juice and 1 t. lemon rind. Refrigerate. When mixture begins to congeal, stir in 2 C. sweetened, cooked rhubarb. Fold in ½ C. whipping cream, whipped stiff. Pour into a 9-inch baked pastry shell or graham cracker crust (recipes at the end of this chapter).

French Peach Cream Pie

Combine: 4 C. sliced, firm-ripe peaches with a mixture of ½ C. sugar, 1 T. flour, ½ t. nutmeg, 1 egg, and 2 T. cream. Mix lightly and pour into a single 9-inch unbaked pie shell.

Crumble together: ¼ C. butter, ½ C. brown sugar, and ½ C. flour and sprinkle over the peaches. Bake at 400 degrees for 35 to 40 minutes.

Grape Parfait Pie

Combine 1¼ C. grape juice (not grape "drink") with 2 T. lemon juice and bring to a boil. Remove from heat and add 1 envelope unflavored gelatin and 1/3 C. sugar. Stir until dissolved. To the grape juice mixture, add 1 pt. vanilla ice cream, spooning in and stirring until melted. Chill until mixture holds its shape on a spoon. Pour into a one-crust 9-inch pie shell (baked and cooled). Chill until set. Decorate with whipped cream, if desired.

Fruit Cocktail Pie

Make a 9-inch graham cracker pie shell according to your favorite recipe (or use mine at the end of this chapter). Reserve 1/3 C. crumbs for top.

In the top of a double boiler, over simmering water, combine ½ lb. (about 16) regular size marshmallows and ½ C. milk. Stir until marshmallows are dissolved. Cool. Add 1 No. 2 can drained fruit cocktail and ½ pt. heavy cream, whipped. (Fold the whipped cream in gently!) Turn into the graham cracker crust and top with the few remaining crumbs. Chill until well set, about 3 hours.

Prune Chiffon Pie

This pie may be made with cooked, dried *apricots* and is perfectly wonderful for flavor variety—just substitute the cooked apricots and juice in place of the prunes and juice!

Dissolve 1 pkg. unflavored gelatin in ¼ C. cold water.

Heat to a boiling point:

1 C. finely chopped, cooked prunes

¾ C. prune juice

½ C. sugar

¼ t. salt

2 T. lemon juice

1 t. grated lemon rind

Add the gelatin and refrigerate. When it begins to set, *fold* in:

2 egg whites, stiffly beaten

Turn into a 9-inch baked pastry shell and chill about 3 hours, or until set. Garnish with whipped cream, if desired.

Dorothy's Pumpkin Ice Cream Pie (Uncooked)

Combine:
1 C. pumpkin
½ C. brown sugar
½ t. salt
½ t. cinnamon
½ t. ginger
¼ t. nutmeg

Soften 1 qt. vanilla ice cream and combine with the pumpkin mixture. Turn into a 9-inch graham cracker crust and *freeze* until serving time.

Serves 6 to 8.

German Sweet Chocolate Pie

In a small saucepan, over low heat, combine 1 4-oz. pkg. German sweet chocolate (Baker's) and ¼ C. butter. Stir constantly until chocolate is melted. Remove from heat and gradually stir in 1 14½ oz. evaporated milk.

Combine:
1½ C. sugar
3 T. cornstarch
⅛ t. salt
2 eggs, beaten
1 t. vanilla

Gradually add the chocolate mixture, mixing all together until well blended. Turn into a 10-inch pie shell.

Mix together;
1 1/3 C. flaked coconut
½ C. pecans, chopped

Sprinkle the coconut-pecan mixture over the chocolate filling and bake at 375 degrees for 45 minutes or until top of pie puffs up. The filling will set as it cools. This pie is very rich and a 10-inch pie will serve 8 to 10 people.

Mama's Lemon Meringue Pie

This is one of those delectables that "shiver" on your fork—perfect consistency!

In the top of a double boiler, combine:

1 C. sugar
5 T. cornstarch
⅛ t. salt
3 egg yolks

Gradually add 2 C. boiling water and the grated rind and juice of 1 lemon. Cook until thickened and add 1 t. butter. Stir well. Pour into a baked 9-inch pie shell and top with a meringue made of the three remaining egg whites.

Meringue: Beat 3 egg whites until frothy. Continue beating while gradually beating in 6 T. sugar, ⅛ t. salt, ¼ t. cream of tartar. Top pie with meringue, sealing well to the crust to prevent shrinkage. Top with grated lemon peel and brown in a 325-degree oven for 9 or 10 minutes, or until delicately brown. Watch carefully!

Serves 6.

Pecan Pie

Cream 1 T. butter with 1 C. brown sugar and 2 T. flour. Add 1 C. light corn syrup and beat until frothy. Add 3 eggs, slightly beaten. Add ¼ t. salt, 1 t. vanilla, and 1 C. pecan halves (or broken pieces). Pour into a 9-inch unbaked pie shell. Bake at 325 degrees for 40 minutes. Easy and so good!

Chocolate Mija Pie

(Such as the one served at famous Bauer's Restaurant in Denver, Colorado)

In a small bowl, combine:

1 C. sugar
4 T. cornstarch
¼ t. salt
¼ C. milk

Blend in 2 egg yolks.

In the top of a double boiler, over simmering water, scald 1½ C. milk. Add the sugar mixture to the scalding milk, stirring constantly. Beat with a rotary beater (or wire whisk) until smooth and clear.

Mix 4 T. cocoa with ¼ C. milk and add to the above. Grate 2 oz. German chocolate and add to above mixture. Continue cooking and stirring until all the chocolate is melted and mixture is thick. Remove from heat. Add ½ t. vanilla. Cool thoroughly. Turn into a 9-inch baked pie shell. Sprinkle with ½ C. Mija candy (ground Heath Bar may be used if Mija candy is unavailable), ground. Chill thoroughly.

Strawberry Chiffon Pie

Soak 1 envelope of unflavored gelatin in ¼ C. cold water for 5 minutes. Separate 4 eggs and beat yolks slightly. To the yolks add ½ C. sugar, 1 T. lemon juice, and ¼ t. salt. Cook in the top of a double boiler, over simmering water, until it has a custard-like consistency. Add the softened gelatin. Stir until dissolved. Add 1 C. fresh, crushed, ripe strawberries, reserving 6 more whole perfect berries for garnish. Stir the strawberries into the first mixture with 3 drops red food coloring. Cool in refrigerator. When mixture begins to congeal, fold in the remaining 4 egg whites, stiffly beaten with ¼ C. sugar.

Turn into a 9-inch baked pie shell and chill 3 or 4 hours. At serving time, whip ½ pt. cream with 2 T. sugar and spread on pie. Garnish with the whole, perfect berries. It will be a family favorite!

Serves 6.

Standard Crust

For a two-crust pie (divide in half for a 9-inch pastry shell).

In a medium bowl, combine with the fingertips (or a pastry blender):

2 C. sifted flour
2/3 C. shortening (vegetable shortening or lard—I use Fluffo)
½ t. salt

When the mixture resembles cornmeal, add cold water, a little at a time, until it holds together in a ball. (Usually 4 to 5 T. cold water is sufficient.) Divide dough in two and flatten, with the hands, into a round on a lightly floured board (or pastry cloth). With a lightly floured rolling pin (covered or uncovered), roll the round into a circle an inch larger than your pie plate. Turn under the overlap and flute with the fingers to make a 1-crust pie, or when making a 2-crust pie, seal bottom and top crusts at pan edge with a little cold water; tuck under top crust and flute in a uniform pattern. (Brushing the top with a bit of milk before baking and sprinkling with a mixture of sugar and cinnamon is nice for most fruit pies as it gives a glaze to the crust.)

Nut Crust (1 8-inch Crust)

Melt ½ C. butter. Combine 1 C. flour, ¼ C. brown sugar, and 1 C. finely chopped nuts. Stir in the melted butter. Put in 8-inch pie plate and bake 15 minutes at 325 degrees. *Remove from pan and stir well.* While warm, press into pan to form a shell, reserving a few crumbs to put on the top of your pie filling.

Graham Cracker Crust (A Single 9-Inch Crust)

Combine all ingredients and press firmly into a 9-inch pie plate, reserving ½ C. of the mixture to sprinkle over top of pie for a garnish.

1½ C. graham cracker crumbs
½ C. melted butter
¼ C. sifted, powdered sugar

This crust may be baked at 350 degrees for 10 minutes. I prefer this, but it is not a "must." Cool crust before adding the filling.

Salad Oil Crust

Mix together 1 1/3 C. sifted flour and ½ t. salt. In a measuring cup, pour 1/3 C. salad oil and 3 T. cold milk (do not stir to mix). Pour, all at once, into the flour mixture. Stir with a fork until mixed. Make into a smooth ball and flatten slightly. Place between two sheets of waxed paper and roll into a circle large enough to fit a 9-inch pie plate. Flute edges and bake as recipe directs for Standard Crust.

Note: Dampen counter under your waxed paper—it won't slip.

Cream Cheese Pastry

This is an excellent pastry for making hors d'oeuvres or tiny filled pies.

Mix 1 3-oz. pkg. cream cheese, softened with ¼ C. butter, ⅛ t. salt, and 1 C. flour. Chill and roll as per your Standard Crust recipe.

Blackberry Pie

Prepare pastry for a two-crust pie. Roll one-half of the pastry to fit a 9-inch pie plate. Roll out second half and cut in strips to weave in a lattice top.

In a large bowl, combine, tossing gently:

4 C. blackberries or black raspberries
¾ C. sugar
2½ T. instant tapioca
Dash salt
⅛ t. nutmeg

Turn into prepared crust. Dot with 2 T. butter. Weave lattice crust. Srinkle with about 1 t. cinnamon-sugar mixture. Bake at 375 degrees for about 50 minutes or until brown and bubbling.

RICE, NOODLE & BARLEY DISHES

Wild Rice With Almonds

The very best of my collection!

In a heavy skillet, melt ¼ C. butter and stir in 1 C. wild rice (natural). Stir over medium heat until rice begins to yellow, then add ½ C. slivered almonds, 6 large fresh mushrooms, cleaned and sliced (or 1 6-oz. can) and 2 T. fresh green onions, sliced. Stir until onions and mushrooms are limp—about 5 minutes. Turn into a 2-qt. casserole. In the skillet, put 3 C. chicken broth (canned is fine). Bring to a boil and turn over the rice mixture in the casserole. (No salt, please!) Cover tightly. Bake at 325 degrees for 1 hour. This dish is great for company, as it keeps well if dinner must wait a little while.

Serves 8.

Noodles Romanoff (Special)

Cook an 8-oz. pkg. small noodles according to package directions. Drain well and combine with the following ingredients:

½ C. cooked, diced bacon
1 C. cottage cheese, cream style
1 C. sour cream
¼ C. onion, finely minced
1 clove garlic, pressed
2 t. worchestershire sauce
½ t. salt
1 T. prepared horseradish
Dash of tabasco sauce

Mix ingredients well. Place in a buttered 1-qt. casserole. Bake at 350 degrees for 30 minutes. Remove from oven and sprinkle with ½ C. grated cheddar cheese and 2 T. parmesan cheese. Return to oven and bake 10 minutes more.

Serves 6. Try this with grilled Bratwurst!

Fried Rice

Cook 1½ C. precooked rice according to package directions. Let stand until you have prepared the following:

Beat 2 eggs with ¼ t. salt and turn into a buttered skillet. Cook over medium heat, turning once, only until set. Remove to a platter and cut in small strips. Reserve.

In the skillet, melt 2 T. butter and add ½ C. chopped green onions, 2 T. green pepper, minced, and ½ C. celery, thinly sliced (diagonally). Cook 3 minutes, stirring constantly. Do not overcook!

Add the rice and 1 to 1½ C. chopped meat (pork, ham, beef, chicken, or tuna). Stir and toss gently to heat through. Add 2 T. soy sauce and the egg strips. Garnish with a bit of chives or onion tops.

Serves 6.

Golden Rice

1 C. precooked rice, cooked according to package directions. Grate 2 medium-size carrots and add the rice during the last 5 minutes "resting" period. Combine with 2 eggs beaten with ½ C. milk, ½ t. salt, ¼ t. pepper, ½ t. dry mustard, 2 T. dried, minced onion, ½ t. parsley (fresh or dried). Gently fold in 1 C. grated cheddar cheese. Bake in a well-buttered 1½-qt. casserole at 350 degrees for 30 minutes. Top with an additional ½ C. grated cheddar cheese and return to oven for 10 minutes. Garnish with parsley and pimiento strips.

Serves 6.

Rice Pilau

Wash 2 C. regular rice in cold water until it is free from starch residue. Drain. In a heavy skillet, in ½ C. butter sauce, saute 1 medium onion finely chopped and 1 clove garlic, pressed, until tender—about 5 minutes. Add the drained rice. Cook and stir 5 minutes longer.

Add 4 C. boiling chicken broth (canned is fine) or water and 6 cloves, 6 cardamon seeds (or ¼ t. powdered cardamon), ⅛ t. powdered allspice, and 1 1-inch piece stick cinnamon and ½ t. ground tumeric. Cover and simmer 30 to 40 minutes, or until all broth is absorbed. Stir with a fork.

In a small skillet, saute ½ C. slivered almonds, stirring constantly until golden brown. Add the almonds to the rice along with ½ C. white or dark seedless raisins and 1 t. salt. Toss together well and serve 6 happy people!

Poppy Seed Noodles

Cook an 8-oz. pkg. fine noodles according to package directions. Drain.

In a skillet, melt 6 T. butter and saute 1 cut clove of garlic for 2 or 3 minutes. Remove garlic. Cut a large slice of unseeded rye bread into small dice and add to the garlic-butter in the skillet. Saute until crisp, stirring constantly. Toss the bread, butter, and cooked noodles with 2 T. poppy seeds.

Serves 6.

Macaroni Loaf (A Custard-Like Loaf)

Cook 1 C. salad-style macaroni (shells or elbow) according to package directions. Drain.

Scald 1 C. milk and pour over 2 C. soft white bread crumbs. Stir well. Add to the macaroni along with 1 C. grated cheddar cheese, ½ C. melted butter, 2 pimientos, diced, 2 T. chopped parsley, 1 t. salt, and 2 T. chopped green pepper.

Separate 4 eggs and beat yolks and whites separately. Add the yolks to the macaroni mixture and fold in the stiffly beaten whites. Turn into a large buttered loaf pan. Put the loaf pan in a pan of hot water and bake at 350 degrees for 45 minutes or until nearly firm. Serve with a sauce made of cream of mushroom soup, thinned with a little milk.

Serves 8.

Gourmet Barley Casserole

In a large skillet, saute 1 C. barley in 3 T. butter until it becomes golden in color. Place in a buttered 1½ qt. casserole. In the same skillet, saute ¾ C. sliced fresh mushrooms in 1 T. butter, add ¼ C. coarsely chopped cashews, and saute 1 minute. Combine with the barley in the casserole. Add 1 C. hot chicken broth (canned is fine). Cover tightly and bake at 350 degrees for 40 minutes. Add 1 more cup of broth, stir barley, bake 40 minutes more. Add 1½ C. broth, again, and bake 25 minutes longer or until broth has been absorbed and barley is puffed. Sprinkle with a few more cashews and serve 4 to 6!

SALADS & SALAD DRESSINGS

One of the most important and interesting parts of a meal is the salad course. With so many marvelous recipes today, there is no need for salad to be uninteresting. You'll be surprised how a bottle of really "homemade" salad dressing will help perk up the family's appetite.

Four Bean Salad

This is an old standby, but the dressing is different and very good. this is a large recipe, but it will keep a week, improving with the long marinading.

In a large collander, put:

1 No. 2 can Blue Lake whole green beans
1 No. 2 can whole wax beans
1 No. 2 can kidney beans, drained and rinsed (red)
1 No. 2 can garbanzo beans

Let the beans drain in the collander while you prepare the dressing. (Discard juices or reserve for the soup pot.)

Thinly slice 1 medium onion; separate into rings. Cut 1 medium green pepper into small dice and 1 medium pimiento, diced (or you may use 2 T. diced, canned pimiento).

In a large mixing bowl, combine the drained beans, onion, pepper, and pimiento.

In a 2-C. measuring cup (or bowl), combine the dressing:

½ C. sugar
½ t. dry mustard
1 t. salt
½ t. dried tarragon leaves, crumbled
½ t. sweet basil, crumbled
½ C. red wine vinegar
½ C. salad oil
2 T. parsley, minced

Mix the dressing thoroughly by beating with a fork. Drizzle over the vegetables and stir gently—do not break beans. Cover and refrigerate overnight (or longer), stirring gently once or twice. At serving time, stir and drain. (Reserve the drained dressing to put back on in case you have leftovers!)

Makes enough to serve 10 to 12 appreciative people.

Cucumber Yogurt

(Use your own homemade yogurt—recipe is in the miscellaneous chapter of this book.)

In a medium-size bowl, coarsely grate 2 medium cucumbers which have been thinly peeled and seeds removed.

Finely mince 3 green onions and 2 T. parsley. Add to the cucumbers.

In another bowl, combine 2 C. yogurt, 2 T. sugar, ½ t. salt, ⅛ t. pepper, and ¼ t. paprika. Stir together, gently. (Beating yogurt will make it thinner. Try to keep the custard-like consistency.) Combine with the cucumbers by folding gently together with a fork. Garnish with a bit more parsely.

Serves 6.

Avocado Ring With Crabmeat Dressing

(Great party salad)

In a large bowl, combine:

4 regular size boxes lemon gelatin
4 C. boiling water

Stir until gelatin is dissolved and add:

2 C. cold water
¼ C. lemon juice
½ t. salt
¼ t. tabasco

Refrigerate. When mixture begins to congeal, add 3 large avocados which have been forced through a sieve, and ¾ C. mayonnaise. Beat with a rotary beater until well blended. Gently stir in 1 C. sour cream and blend well. Pour into a 3-qt. ring (or other mold). Chill overnight or several hours, until firm. Unmold on a large plate, surrounded with salad greens. Garnish with additional avocado slices and wedges of firm ripe tomatoes. If you use a ring mold, put the dressing in a footed sherbet dish, or compote, and put in center of ring—otherwise, serve dressing in a side dish.

Crabmeat Dressing

Combine:
1½ C. mayonnaise
1/3 C. milk
1/3 C. chili sauce
1 T. lemon juice
1 6-oz. pkg. frozen crab meat, thawed and flaked

Mix together well. Garnish top of dressing with a bit of minced parsley leaves.

Serves 12.

Chop Suey Salad With Chinese Noodles

In a large bowl, combine:

2 C. cooked chicken or turkey
1 C. celery, diced
3 T. minced onion
2 hardcooked eggs, diced
1/3 C. walnuts, coarsely broken
¼ C. sweet pickle relish

In a measuring cup, mix:
2/3 C. mayonnaise
2 T. vinegar
1 T. worchestershire sauce
1 t. salt
⅛ t. pepper
1 T. parsley, minced

Turn the dressing over the chicken (or turkey) mixture and chill well. At serving time, add 1 C. crisp Chinese noodles and mix together well. Serve on crisp lettuce cups.

Serves 6. (This is a fine salad, but do not add noodles in advance, as they should not lose their crispness!)

Mom Hoegh's Orange Salad

Bring 1 C. mandarin orange juice to a full boil. Add 1 pkg. orange gelatin and stir until gelatin is dissolved. Cool 5 minutes, then spoon 1 pint of orange sherbet into the gelatin mixture. Add 1 C. drained mandarin oranges (chilled). Pour into a shallow 8-by-8-inch square dish. Chill. When well set, cut in rectangles, and serve on a lettuce cup with a dob of mayonnaise, mixed with a bit of sour cream.

Serves 6.

Nellie's "Different" Salad

In the top of a double boiler, heat 1 C. tomato soup over simmering water. Add 1 3-oz. pkg. cream cheese.

In a small pan, heat to boiling ½ C. water. Add 1 pkg. (regular) lemon gelatin. Stir until gelatin is dissolved and add to the soup-cream cheese mixture. Stir well. Add ½ C. cold water. Remove from heat. Cool.

When cook, but not set, stir in:

½ C. mayonnaise
½ C. celery, finely diced
1 medium onion, grated
½ medium green pepper, diced
½ C. cucumber, diced fine
¼ C. stuffed green olives, sliced
Dash of salt
½ t. worchestershire sauce

Combine well and pour into 6 or 8 individual molds (or 1 large mold). Chill until well set.

Serves 6 to 8 on crisp lettuce.

Orange-Onion Salad

This is so simple and delicious. Don't be afraid of the combination—it's great.

On a crispy slice of lettuce, arrange alternate slices of peeled, seedless oranges (cut away any tough membrane) and thinly sliced red (or sweet, white) onions. Drizzle with "Russian Dressing" (recipe included at end of this chapter).

Avocado-Grapefruit Salad

Another simple, elegant salad!

Peel and slice in medium-thick slices 2 large avocados. Peel one large grapefuit, section, and remove membrane with a sharp knife. Arrange alternately on crisp lettuce and sprinkle with a few pomegranate seeds, if available. (The seeds are not necessary but add a great deal to the attractiveness of this salad!)

Serves 4. Serve with Russian or French Dressing (recipes included at the end of this chapter).

Cardinal Salad

Dissolve 1 pkg. lemon gelatin in 1 C. boiling water. Stir until dissolved. Add ¾ C. beet juice. Stir well and add:

1 C. cooked, diced beets
½ t. salt
1 T. vinegar
1 T. horseradish
¾ C. celery, finely diced
2 T. grated onion

When the combination begins to congeal, stir to prevent settling of the vegetables. Pour into a mold. Chill until well set. Serve with dressing made by combining ¾ C. sour cream, ¼ C. mayonnaise, and 2 t. horseradish. Serve on crisp lettuce leaves to 4 or 6.

Bee's Mustard Ring

This is a truly different salad—make it in a ring mold, and surround with cabbage salad to which a few caraway seeds have been added. You'll need no additional dressing.

In the top of a double boiler, combine:

¾ C. sugar
2 t. dry mustard
¾ C. wine vinegar
¼ C. cold water
4 eggs, well beaten
⅛ t. salt

Cook over simmering water until thick and creamy. In 1 T. cold water, soften 1 pkg. plain gelatin. When soft, add to the hot custard mixture. Cool. Pour into a 1½-qt. mold and chill until well set.

To make the cabbage salad:

Finely shred 1 medium head of cabbage and place in a large bowl. Cover with ice water and refrigerate for 1 hour. Drain well and pat with a clean tea towel to remove excess water.

Grate a medium onion and add to the cabbage. Sprinkle the mixture with ¾ t. salt and 2 T. sugar. Allow to stand in refrigerator for 1 hour. At serving time, thin ½ C. Miracle Whip with 3 T. milk. Turn over the cabbage and toss lightly. Add 1 t. caraway seeds, if desired, and serve on a large serving plate with mustard ring in center. Fill the ring with plum tomatoes or a large bouquet of fresh parsley to finish your "picture."

Serves 8 to 10.

Bee's Corn Salad

A great picnic dish—to pass.

Combine:

1 No. 2 can whole kernel corn
2 T. green pepper, finely diced
1 large pimiento, diced
1 T. onion, minced fine
2 hardcooked eggs, chopped
½ t. salt
⅛ t. pepper
1 clove garlic, pressed (if desired)
2 T. parsley, minced fine
½ C. mayonnaise and 1 T. vinegar

Chill well and serve in a pretty bowl which has been lined with crisp greens.

Serves 6.

Caesar Salad

In a large salad bowl, place 2 large heads of washed and crisped Romaine leaves which have been broken into bite-size pieces. (This may be done ahead and refrigerated.)

Prepare dressing (ahead of time for serving) by combining:

¾ C. salad oil
1 clove garlic, pressed
2 T. wine vinegar
¼ t. dry mustard
¼ t. worchestershire sauce
Juice of ½ lemon (about 1½ T.)

Place ingredients in a jar and shake well. Rinse 6 whole anchovies with hot water, drain on a paper towel, and chop fine. At serving time, add the anchovies to the salad dressing and turn over the salad greens. (There should be enough to coat the greens without leaving a pool of dressing in the bottom of the serving bowl.) Break a raw egg over the top of the salad and toss well. Sprinkle with 1/3 C. grated parmesan cheese and several generous grinds of fresh black pepper. Over the top of all, sprinkle 1 C. toasted croutons.

Serve with pride to 6 or 8 hungry people!

Blue Cheese-Waldorf Salad

So good, it's nearly dessert!

Combine:

1 C. celery, diced
2 C. diced, unpeeled apples
½ C. walnuts, coarsely broken
¼ C. crumbled blue cheese
¼ C. sour cream
¼ C. mayonnaise
Dash salt

Mix well; serve immediately on crisp salad greens.

Serves 6.

Asparagus Luncheon Salad

Cook 1 lb. fresh green asparagus until barely tender (about 5 minutes) in slightly salted water. Drain and chill. Slice (and halve each slice) two large tomatoes. Slice 2 or 3 hardboiled eggs. Arrange the asparagus spears, tomato slices, and sliced eggs on crisp lettuce leaves on 6 individual salad plates. Serve with French dressing or thin 1 C. "Mama's Boiled Dressing" with 3 T. thin cream. (Dressing recipes are both included at the end of this chapter.)

Salad Dressings

Leone's Russian Dressing

In a quart jar, combine the following ingredients and shake well. Shake before using. Makes 1 qt.

¾ C. sugar
½ C. salad oil
2/3 C. vinegar
1 10½-oz. can tomato soup
1 t. salt
1 t. dry mustard
1 t. paprika
1 medium onion, grated
1 medium green pepper, ground

Lemon-Honey Fruit Dressing

Combine:
1 C. mayonnaise
4 T. honey
3 T. lemon juice
½ t. grated lemon rind
½ t. celery seed

Makes about 1¼ C. dressing for fruits.

Mama's Boiled Dressing

Wonderful for cabbage or potato salad.

Combine in the top of a double boiler:

2¼ T. flour
1 t. mustard
½ C. sugar
1 t. salt
½ t. paprika
½ C. cider vinegar
1 C. water

Cook over simmering water until it begins to thicken. In a bowl, beat 2 whole eggs (remove the "strings" from the whites and discard). Add 4 T. of the hot mixture to the beaten eggs, then add the egg mixture gradually to the mixture in the double boiler. Cook 5 minutes more, stirring constantly. (Thin with a bit of sweet or sour cream at serving time.)

Yield: 2 cups.

Blue Cheese Dressing

Perfect dressing for a wedge of lettuce!

Combine and stir well:

3 oz. blue cheese, crumbled fine
¼ t. garlic salt
½ C. salad oil
¼ C. vinegar
1 C. sour cream

Makes about 2 cups.

Bee's French Dressing

Best I've ever tasted!

In a blender, combine:

½ C. sugar
1 C. salad oil
2/3 C. catsup
½ C. vinegar
2 t. salt
2 t. paprika
1 medium onion, grated

Blend at medium speed for 3 minutes (or shake in a quart jar). Makes 2½ C. of delicious dressing.

Low-Calorie Roquefort Dressing

Crumble 1 wedge (about 1½ oz.) Roquefort cheese in a medium-size bowl.

Add:
2 C. thick buttermilk
1 C. mayonnaise (or low-cal. salad dressing)
½ t. salt
Several grinds fresh black pepper
3 T. onion, grated
1 clove garlic, crushed

Beat well with a fork. Makes 3 C. dressing.

Blender Cranberry Fruit Dressing

In blender, combine:

1 C. sugar
1 t. salt
1 t. dry mustard
½ C. vinegar
1 t. onion juice
1 C. salad oil
1 unpeeled orange, cut up and seeded
1 C. cranberries, raw and washed

Turn on blender and blend for 2 or 3 minutes at medium speed. Makes about 3 cups of delicious dressing. Try it on a pear salad for extra-special delight!

Borsch French Dressing

In a small bowl, combine:

1 C. salad oil
½ C. wine vinegar
½ t. salt
⅛ t. pepper
½ t. worchestershire sauce
½ t. paprika

In a second medium bowl, place:

¼ C. chopped parsley
2 T. minced onion
2 hardboiled eggs, minced fine
½ C. finely chopped beets

Combine ingredients, stirring well.

Yield: 2 cups.

SANDWICHES HOT & COLD

I do hope the following recipes will become favorites with your family and friends. Each recipe is unique enough to spark a "jaded" appetite.

"Teen" Dogs

Your teenagers can eat two a piece—so make plenty!

For 8 sandwiches, use:

8 wiener buns, lightly buttered

Mix:

6 wieners, chopped
1 C. grated cheddar cheese
3 hardcooked eggs, chopped
½ C. green stuffed olives
¾ C. mayonnaise
½ C. chili sauce
2 T. sweet pickle relish, drained

Combine and divide among the wiener buns. Wrap each filled bun in a square of aluminum foil and place on a cookie sheet. Bake at 400 degrees for 20 minutes. (Your teenagers can do this themselves and will enjoy the delightful results!)

Sloppy Joes With Variations

BASIC RECIPE:

Saute together in 1 T. salad oil:

2 lbs. ground beef
1 medium onion, chopped

Add:

½ C. catsup
1 T. prepared mustard
1 can chicken gumbo soup, undiluted
1 3-oz. can mushroom pieces, drained

Cook all together for 30 minutes over low heat. Add 1 t. salt and ¼ t. pepper. Serve on 6 sandwich rolls.

VARIATIONS:

Italian Style: Substitute 1 can minestrone soup (undiluted) for the chicken gumbo and add ¼ t. crushed oregano.

Beef Onion: Substitute 1 can onion soup (undiluted) for the chicken gumbo; add 2 T. flour and cook 3 minutes.

Mushroom Joes: Prepare meat and onions as above. For the remaining ingredients, substitute the following: ¼ C. mushroom soup, 2/3 C. soft bread crumbs, ½ t. grated onion, and 1 egg. Form into 8 bun-size patties and saute until brown on both sides, in 2 T. fat. Add ¼ C. water to the remainder of the can of mushroom soup and turn over the patties. Cook 5 minutes or until thoroughly heated. Serve on 8 hamburger buns which have been sparingly buttered and lightly toasted.

Creole Joes: Prepare the meat and onions as in the Basic Recipe. Stir in 1 can pepper pot soup, undiluted, along with 2 T. catsup, 1 t. prepared mustard, 1 t. minced parsley, and ½ t. gumbo file (optional but very fine!). Serve on toasted buns. Makes 8.

Heavenly Burger Bake for 12

Lightly toast 24 slices of white bread and spread with 4 T. margarine or butter.

Brown 1½ lbs. ground chuck in 2 T. fat with:

¾ C. diced onion
¼ C. minced celery

Add:
3 T. prepared mustard
1 T. diced pimiento

Arrange 12 slices of the toast in a large, shallow baking pan. Spread the meat filling over the slices. Sprinkle over all 3 C. grated cheddar cheese. Cover with second slice of toast.

Beat 6 eggs slightly. Add 2½ C. milk and ½ t. salt. Pour egg and milk combination over all. Bake at 350 degrees for 40 minutes.

Serve with tomato slices on lettuce with a simple dressing for a complete meal!

Serves 12.

French Salmon Loaf Sandwich

Cut a small loaf of French bread in two, lengthwise, and remove the soft part of the bread to a large mixing bowl. Butter the crust section, on both sides, with 3 T. softened butter.

In a saucepan, saute ¼ C. finely minced onion and ¼ C. minced celery. Add to the soft bread. Remove skin, bones, and liquid from a 7¾-oz. can of red salmon and flake the meat. Combine with the bread crumbs, adding 1 C. grated cheddar cheese, 1 t. prepared mustard, 2 T. chopped stuffed green olives, and 2 hardcooked eggs, chopped. Fill the bread shells with the mixture and place tops and bottoms together. Wrap the loaf in aluminum foil. Bake at 375 degrees for 25 minutes. Makes 4 or 5 generous slices.

Party Loaf

This is a sandwich loaf that should be done the "day-before-the-party" as it needs to "set up." Frost the morning of the party—keep all well chilled.

Have a loaf of white sandwich bread prepared by your bakery (or do it yourself). Have crusts removed and the loaf sliced in 5 slices, *lengthwise*. Spread each long slice, very lightly, with very soft butter. Spread each slice with *all* of the following fillings:

Egg Salad: Mix 3 hardcooked eggs, finely chopped, with 3 slices cooked, crumbled bacon, ½ t. grated onion, 1 t. chili sauce, and 4 T. mayonnaise.

Salmon Salad: Mix 1 7¾-oz. can red salmon, ½ C. finely minced celery, 1 T. finely minced green, stuffed olives, and 4 T. mayonnaise.

Ham Salad: 1 C. finely minced ham, 2 T. green pepper, finely minced, ½ t. prepared mustard, ¼ t. worchestershire sauce, and 4 T. mayonnaise.

Pineapple-Cheese: 1 3-oz. pkg. cream cheese, ½ C. cheddar cheese, grated, and ½ C. drained, crushed pineapple.

Stack layers together. Wrap in waxed paper and chill until firm—about 4 hours (or overnight).

About 3 hours before serving time, combine 1 8-oz. pkg. cream cheese and ¼ C. cream. Place the loaf on a large cold serving platter and frost with the cream cheese mixture. Decorate with olive slices, parsley, and pimientos. Use your imagination! This loaf will serve about 30 ½-slices. Be sure to keep cold for easy cutting.

Pronto Puppies

In a medium-size saucepan, put 1 1-lb. package (from 8 to 11 frankfurters) and cover with cold water. Bring slowly to the boiling point, reduce heat, and allow to hold just under boiling for 10 minutes. Meanwhile, prepare batter and start 1 qt. salad oil heating in your deep-fat fryer.

For batter, combine:

6 T. flour
3 T. yellow cornmeal
¼ t. baking powder
½ t. salt
½ t. sugar
4 T. milk
1 T. water
1 egg, well beaten

Beat together. Drain hot frankfurters; cool slightly. Dip each frankfurter, with a sharp fondue fork stuck in the end, into batter. Fry in deep fat until golden brown. For serving, stick a skewer into end of each. Serve with catsup, mustard, or a combination of both.

Makes 8 to 11 puppies.

Delicious Pork Barbecue (For Buns)

Cut 2 lbs. lean pork shoulder in 1-inch cubes and brown in 1 T. butter. Add ½ C. water, cover closely, and cook until very tender (about ½ hour). Add 1 C. catsup, 1/3 C. water, 1 T. sugar, 1 T. vinegar, 1 t. dry mustard, and 1 t. mixed pickling spice (tied in a bag). Cook very slowly for 1 hour or until sauce thickens. Serve on hot buns.

Serves 6. (Remove spice bag!)

Eddie's "Kookie" Special

Lightly butter 6 slices of bread. Spread peanut butter on 6 slices of bread. Spread the peanut-buttered slices with sandwich spread (pickle-type). Lay on the sandwich spread, sliced lunchmeat (your favorite—but big bologna or liverwurst are fine!). Cover each of the six slices with a thin slice of tomato and a lettuce leaf. Cover with the first 6 slices of bread.

Serve to 6 hungry "big-mouthed" people!

P.S. Eddie's special is excellent *grilled* on a hot griddle before adding the tomato and lettuce. In that case, omit the inside buttering and lightly butter both sides of the outside sandwich before grilling!

SAUCES

My Best Barbecue

In a medium saucepan, combine:

3 T. brown sugar
½ t. salt
1 t. dry mustard
½ t. chili powder
1 C. catsup
1 medium onion, grated
½ t. curry powder
1 t. celery seed
¼ C. wine vinegar
1 C. red burgundy wine
1 T. worchestershire sauce
¼ T. Wright's Liquid Smoke

Cook all together, over low heat, for 1 hour or until thick and has a glazed appearance. Try this for rotisserie cooking. During the last 30 to 40 minutes, baste meat every 5 minutes using a pastry brush. (Meat may be rolled roast of beef, turkey, pork loin—or it's good for basting grilled hamburgers, too!)

Makes about 3 cups.

Dorothy's Barbecue Sauce

Marvelous for spareribs and it makes a gallon. Freeze what you don't need. Turn into pint containers, cool, and freeze as usual.

In a preserving kettle, combine the following ingredients:

1 No. 10 can tomato catsup
2 C. salad oil
¾ C. brown sugar
2 C. cider vinegar
3 cloves garlic, pressed
2 T. chili powder
1 t. dry mustard
4 bay leaves
1 t. salt
¼ t. pepper
½ t. crushed, dried oregano
2 T. hot pepper sauce
1 t. crushed dried rosemary

Cook slowly for 1 hour or until slightly thickened. Add 2 t. liquid smoke (Wright's). Cool. Use as indicated. Makes 8 pts. Wonderful to have on hand!

Mustard Sauce

Excellent with fish or ham.

In the top of a double boiler, combine:

1 boullion cube
1 C. hot water
½ C. sugar
½ C. vinegar
¼ C. prepared salad mustard
¼ C. butter
1½ T. flour
3 egg yolks, well beaten

Cook over simmering water, stirring constantly until thick. Cool. Store, covered, in the refrigerator.

Makes about 2 cups.

Apricot Barbecue Sauce

Force 1 C. of canned apricots, drained through a sieve. Combine with ¼ C. wine vinegar, ¼ C. salad oil, ¼ C. catsup, 2 T. brown sugar, 2 T. grated onion, ¼ t. worchestershire sauce, ½ t. salt, and a dash of tabasco sauce. Bring to a boil in a small saucepan and cook 5 to 10 minutes until well blended. (This is a fine sauce for barbecueing turkey, chicken, or pork roast!)

Makes 1½ cups sauce.

Mustard-Kumquat Sauce

Serve cold on beef, tongue, or turkey.

In a blender, puree 3 large preserved kumquats with ¼ C. juice from the jar of kumquats, 1 T. lemon juice, and 1 t. dry mustard. When well blended, fold gently into ¼ C. plain yogurt. Serve well chilled.

Piquant Sauce for Vegetables

Marvelous sauce for asparagus or broccoli.

In the top of a double boiler, combine:

1 3-oz. pkg. cream cheese
¼ t. salt
¼ t. dry mustard
2 drops worchestershire sauce
1 whole egg (remove "string" from white)
1 T. lemon juice.

Cook over simmering water, beating with a rotary beater until thickened. With a spoon, stir in ½ C. sour cream. Serve warm over cooked asparagus or broccoli. This sauce is also excellent for cabbage cooked tender crisp (about 5 minutes), adding ½ t. caraway seed!

Makes about ¾ C. sauce.

Honey-Ginger Sauce for Ice Cream

In a small saucepan, combine:

2 C. honey
½ C. water
⅛ t. salt
½ C. candied ginger, finely minced

Bring to a boil and cook slowly for 5 minutes. Add 1 C. pecans, coarsely chopped.

Makes 2½ C. sauce.

Fresh Lingonberry Sauce

Elegant on Sour Dough Pancakes (recipe included in this cookbook).

Wash and measure 4 C. fresh lingonberries into a medium-size saucepan. Add 1 C. water and 1 C. sugar. Cook gently for 10 minutes. Sauce thickens as it stands. Good on ice cream, too.

Orange Syrup (for Waffles)

Add the grated rind of 3 large oranges and 2 C. sugar to 1 C. of boiling water. Stir until sugar is dissolved. Cover and set aside (at room temperature) *for 2 days*! Pour this syrup into a saucepan, add ½ C. fresh orange juice, and a dash of salt; bring to boil and boil 5 minutes. Strain into a large syrup pitcher. Serve warm with melted butter for waffles or pancakes (fine for baba cakes, also!)

Walnut Mocha Sauce for Ice Cream

In a medium-size saucepan, combine ¾ C. evaporated milk and 1 6-oz. pkg. chocolate chips. Stir constantly until chocolate chips are melted and sauce is smooth. Add 2 T. instant coffee crystals. Add ½ C. chopped walnuts. Remove from heat and cool. May be served warm or cold over ice cream.

Makes 1¼ C. sauce.

SOUPS & STEWS

Soup, soup, beautiful soup! Nothing puts the family in such a mellow mood as a steaming bowl of soup. My mother always made vegetable soup with "boiling meat" on wash day because it could cook all morning on the back of our wood range that she heated the wash water on! One of my fondest memories of home—the smell of soup simmering and mama's fresh bread baking!

Mama's Soup Recipe

In a large kettle (preferably a big cast iron pot), put 2 lbs. boiling beef and 1 ox tail, cut in joint sections (about 1 lb.). Cover with cold water and bring to a boil. When a scum rises to the top of the water, remove from heat and skim with a metal spoon. (It may be necessary to do this several times and it's very important to a clear broth.) When the broth is clear, add 2 t. salt and cook slowly for 1½ hours, or until meat is fork tender. (The exact kind and quantity of vegetables is not specified, but here is a good guide.)

Prepare vegetables and dice in reasonably uniform pieces:

3 carrots, peeled thinly and diced
3 stalks celery, diced
1 large onion, minced
1 or 2 sprigs parsley, snipped
4 T. canned tomatoes (not the juice)
1 small rutabaga, diced
1 potato, diced
2 T. pearl barley

Remove the meat to a platter and dice—discard bone and cartilage and fat, if any. There should be about 2 to 2½ qts. broth in the kettle. Add the vegetables and simmer slowly for 30 minutes. Return the meat to the kettle and cook slowly 30 minutes longer. Taste for salt—add, if necessary. (This soup can be made the day before and be kept refrigerated—it is really better for standing!)

Makes about 3 qts. delicious soup.

Clam Chowder, My Way

Dice 8 slices bacon and put them in a heavy saucepan (or Dutch oven). Fry until crisp, spooning off fat as it accumulates. Remove bacon and drain on paper toweling. Reserve.

Remove all fat from pan. Return 2 T. bacon fat to pan and to it add 2 large onions, diced fine. Saute until limp but not brown. Add 3 C. diced potatoes, 1 C. water, and 1 8-oz. bottle of clam juice, ½ t. salt, and ¼ t. pepper. Cover tightly and cook slowly for 1 hour.

Add reserved bacon, 2 7½-oz. cans of minced clams (or baby whole clams) and 1 (more) 8-oz. bottle clam juice. Heat slowly to boiling point—turn off heat. Correct the seasoning (additional salt may be needed, but it depends on the salt content of the bacon).

Crumble 4 soda crackers and stir into the chowder. Allow to stand 5 minutes—stir again. Your guests and family will want more than one helping, so I will only say that this amount will serve 4 generously.

New England Lamb Stew

Combine 3 T. flour, 1½ t. salt, and ¼ t. pepper. Have 2 lbs. of lamb shoulder cut in cubes. Roll the cubed lamb in the flour mixture and shake off excess.

In a heavy kettle, melt 2 T. salad oil and brown the meat cubes slowly. When nicely brown on all sides, add:

1 C. bottled cranberry juice
½ C. water
4 T. red table wine
½ C. minced onion
1 clove garlic, pressed
½ C. diced celery
2 t. sugar
½ t. salt

Cover and cook slowly for 1½ hours or until meat is very tender. Then add:

6 small carrots, cut in chunks
8 small boiling onions
4 medium potatoes, quartered

Cover and cook 30 minutes. Add ½ pkg. of frozen green peas; cook 5 minutes. Stir together 1 T. flour and ¼ C. water and thicken the stew just slightly.

Serves 4 to 6.

Christmas Soup

Quick and colorful!

Combine:

1 can tomato-rice soup, undiluted
1 7½-oz. can minced clams
1½ C. water
1 t. parsley, minced

Heat slowly and when it reaches the boiling point, remove from heat. Turn into 4 soup cups and garnish with ½ small avocado, diced.

Serves 4.

Mama's Tomato Stew and Dumplings

Cook 1 qt. fresh, peeled tomatoes, cut up (canned may be used, but fresh are better) with 1 t. lemon juice, 1 t. salt, 1 T. sugar, and ⅛ t. pepper for 15 minutes over low heat. Add ¼ C. butter and 1 beef boullion cube. Bring to the boiling point and carefully place small dumplings on the hot tomatoes. Cover closely and steam 20 minutes without removing cover. Preparing dumplings in the following manner:

Mix together:

1 C. flour

2 t. baking powder

½ t. salt

⅛ t. paprika

Work in 2 T. butter. When mixture resembles cornmeal, add ½ C. milk (less 1 T.). Mix lightly only until dry ingredients are moistened. Pat into a ½-inch-thick round and cut into small bite-size biscuits (use a juice glass, dipped in flour).

Recipe serves 4.

Would you like to have your very own "Cream of Tomato Soup" on your "winter supply" shelf? Here is my mama's *canning* recipe which makes about 10 qts. of delectable soup and can be thinned with an equal amount of milk or cream.

In a large preserving kettle, combine:

14 qts. tomatoes, washed and cut up
14 sprigs parsley, snipped
14 stalks celery, washed and diced
2 whole cloves
1 bay leaf

Cook all together, stirring frequently over low heat until vegetables are tender. Cool slightly and run through a collander or sieve. If you have a blender (my mama didn't), remove cloves and bay leaf and run in blender until well blended. Return to the kettle and add 14 T. flour mixed with enough water to make a thin paste. Add 14 T. butter, 8 T. sugar, 5 T. salt, and a dash of red pepper, and stir constantly until the mixture boils. Continue cooking until the consistency of commercially canned soup (about 1½ hours) over low heat. Pour into sterilized jars and seal as usual. Hot water bath for 20 minutes.

Avocado-Yogurt Soup (Cold)

Force 4 medium-size ripe avocados through a sieve. Combine with 3 t. lime juice, 1 t. grated onion, and 1½ C. canned beef broth. Stir in 2 C. cold yogurt and blend well. Chill before serving.

Serves 6.

STUFFING

Nabisco Stuffing

In a large bowl, crumble enough Nabisco Shredded Wheat biscuits to measure 4 cups.

Heat, in a small skillet, ¼ C. butter and in it saute:

¾ C. finely diced celery
¼ C. finely diced onion

When vegetables are tender, add 3 T. parsley, chopped, 1 C. cooked rice, 1 t. poultry seasoning, ½ t. salt, ¼ t. pepper, 1 egg, beaten, and enough hot water to moisten (½ to ¾ C.). Enough dressing for a small roasting chicken or 4 rock cornish game hens.

Wild Rice Stuffing

Saute 2 large onions, minced in ½ C. butter. Add ½ C. chopped celery leaves, 1 T. parsley, 1 t. sage. Cook 3 minutes. Add 1½ C. raw wild rice, 4 C. hot chicken broth (canned), 1½ t. salt, ⅛ t. pepper. Mix well. Gently simmer 35 to 40 minutes or until rice is tender and broth is absorbed. Cool.

Stuffs a 5-lb. bird or use for "Veal Birds."

Pecan-Corn Bread Stuffing

In a large bowl, combine:

4 C. corn bread
2 C. day-old white bread
¾ C. pecans, chopped (not too fine)
¾ t. salt
⅛ t. pepper
½ t. powdered sage

In a small fry pan, saute in 2 T. butter:

1 C. diced celery
1 medium onion, minced

Add to the dry ingredients. Dice 1 hardboiled egg and add. Combine 1 beaten egg and 1 to 1½ C. chicken broth (enough to moisten the dry ingredients). This is enough for a 5- or 6-lb. chicken or it may be baked in a greased casserole at 325 degrees for 1 hour.

VEGETABLES

Vegetables can really be an exciting main dish or something to enhance the main course. At any rate, let's try to get over the idea that vegetables are the uninteresting but necessary evil at the dinner table. I hope that a few of these recipes will do that for you!

Scalloped Potatoes

This recipe may not look unusual, but it is really very easy and eliminates the need of thickening.

Into a large saucepan, slice raw white potatoes. Add onion (as much as you like). Add whole milk—enough to come just to the top of potatoes and onion. Heat to boiling point over medium heat, *stirring constantly.* (This causes the potato starch to thicken the mixture!) Salt and pepper to taste. Cheese or ham or a combination of both may be added.

Bake 40 to 45 minutes at 325 degrees.

Sweet Potatoes De Luxe

Mash smooth 6 medium, cooked sweet potatoes (canned may be used nicely).

Add:
1½ t. salt
⅛ t. pepper
¼ C. evaporated milk
3 T. butter
¼ C. pecans, chopped coarsely

Mix well and put into a greased 1½-qt. casserole. Bake at 350 degrees for 35 minutes. Cover with marshmallow halves; bake 5 or 6 minutes more—until marshmallows puff and brown lightly.

Serves 6.

Pink Beans

Quick and different!

To 1 No. 2 can cut Blue Lake green beans, add 2 t. grated onion, ¼ t. salt, dash pepper, and 1 10½-oz. can of tomato bisque soup. Turn into a small casserole. Sprinkle with ¼ C. crushed corn chips. Bake 25 minutes at 325 degrees or until well heated.

Serves 4 to 6.

Copenhagen Limas

Cook 1 10-oz. pkg. frozen limas according to directions. Drain.

Heat ¼ C. milk with 1 cut clove garlic. Stir and remove garlic and discard. Add ¼ C. crumbled blue cheese to the milk and add limas. Stir until cheese melts, forming a delicious sauce. Serve in a heated bowl and sprinkle with hot buttered bread crumbs.

Serves 4 to 6.

Sweet and Sour Green Beans

Cook 1 10-oz. pkg. frozen French cut green beans according to directions. Drain. Fry 3 slices bacon, diced, until well crisped. Drain bacon and discard all but 1 T. of the fat in the pan. To it, add 1/3 C. diced onion. Combine with the cooked beans and saute 3 minutes. Add ¼ C. sugar, ¼ C. vinegar, ¼ t. salt, ⅛ t. pepper. Toss gently. Serve hot.

Serves 4 to 6.

Brussels Sprouts in Onion Cream

Cook 1 15-oz. pkg. frozen brussels sprouts according to directions. Drain. Saute ¼ C. chopped green onions in 2 T. butter. Stir in 1 C. sour cream and heat, stirring constantly. Do *not* boil. Add to brussels sprouts and mix well.

Serves 4 to 6.

Carrot Loaf with Tomato Sauce (A Main Dish)

Combine:

1 C. cooked carrots, chopped fine
1 C. walnuts, chopped fine
1 C. soft bread crumbs
1 medium onion, grated
½ stalk celery, minced
2 T. butter
½ t. salt
2 eggs, well beaten

Mix well and turn into a greased loaf pan. Bake at 350 degrees for 30 to 35 minutes or until well set. Let cool to set up for 5 minutes before serving.

In the meantime, prepare the sauce:

In a small saucepan, melt 1 T. butter. Stir in 1 T. flour and add 1 C. canned tomatoes, ¼ t. sweet basil, crushed, a few grains powdered cloves, ¼ t. salt, ⅛ t. pepper. Cook 10 minutes on slow heat. Unmold carrot loaf on a warmed platter and turn the sauce over it. Tuck ends with parsley and serve 4 to 6.

Scalloped Tomatoes

Only the method is different!

Remove thin slices from crusts of 6 slices white bread. *Butter* the bread; break bread into small pieces and put into a 1½-qt. baking dish. Heat 2 C. thick canned tomatoes (or drain off part of juice) with 6 T. brown sugar, ½ t. salt, ½ t. dried sweet basil. Pour the hot tomatoes over the buttered bread. Stir gently and bake at 425 degrees for 30 minutes.

Serves 4 to 5.

3-Bean Barbecue

In a large skillet, saute in 1/3 C. butter:

½ C. onion, minced
1 clove garlic, pressed

Add:
1 T. brown sugar
1 t. dry mustard
¼ C. catsup
1 T. wine vinegar
½ t. salt
⅛ t. pepper
1 1-lb. can Boston baked beans
1 No. 2 can kidney or pinto beans
1 No. 2 can lima beans, drained

Turn into a 2-qt. casserole. Bake at 350 degrees for 30 minutes.

Serves 8.

Batter-Fried Cauliflower

Wash and trim a medium-size head of cauliflower. Make a few gashes across bottom of stalk and cook in boiling salted water until stalk part pierces with a sharp-tined fork. Drain well and cool slightly. Separate into flowerettes. Prepare batter by combining:

1 C. sifted flour
¼ t. salt
⅛ t. baking powder
1 beaten egg
¾ C. milk
1 T. salad oil

Beat together until smooth. Dip caulifl owerettes in batter. Fry in hot deep fat at 375 degrees until golden brown.

Serves about 6.

Pineapple-Beets

Combine, in a medium saucepan:

2 T. brown sugar
1 T. cornstarch
¼ t. salt
⅛ t. cloves
1 T. lemon juice (or vinegar)
1 T. butter

Add 1 C. (1 9-oz. can) pineapple tidbits and juice. Cook together, stirring constantly until mixture thickens. Add 1 1-lb. can baby beets (or julienne-cut), drained, and heat thoroughly.

Serves 6.

Deviled Cabbage

In a large saucepan, combine:

1 1½-lb. head cabbage, shredded fine
2 C. thinly sliced celery

Cover with boiling water. Cook 3 minutes. Drain well. Add 1 can cream of celery soup, 1 T. prepared horseradish, ¼ t. prepared mustard, ½ t. salt, ⅛ t. pepper. Stir well and turn into a buttered 1½-qt. casserole. Top with 1 C. buttered dry bread crumbs (made by combining, in a small skillet, 1 C. dry crumbs with ¼ C. butter. Stir until delicately brown). Bake 25 minutes at 350 degrees.

Serves 6.

Sweet and Sour Red Cabbage

Shred 1 medium head red cabbage (about 3 lbs.). Put into a large saucepan with ½ C. water, 2 tart apples, peeled and sliced thin, 1 medium onion, chopped, ¼ C. vinegar, ¼ C. sugar, 2 T. bacon fat, 1 t. salt, and ¼ t. pepper. Bring to a boil. Reduce heat and cook, covered, for ½ hour. Sprinkle with 1 T. flour and stir until thickened, about 5 minutes.

Serves 6.

Stuffed Mushrooms

Elegant!

Use large mushrooms. If very large, trim and peel the caps. If medium sized, wash with a small brush. Break off the stems from the caps and reserve. In a medium saucepan, melt ¼ C. butter (or more, if needed) and add 1 t. lemon juice. Toss the caps in the butter to coat well. Put the caps in a shallow buttered baking dish, and fill the cavity with the following mixture:

In the pan in which you tossed the caps, add a bit more butter and saute the *chopped* mushroom stems, about 10 minutes, stirring constantly. Add leftover crab, lobster, chicken, pork (or chicken spread will do—but crab is best). Add a bit of pressed garlic clove, a few drops worchestershire sauce, a few soft bread crumbs, and 1 beaten egg. Heap on the caps; sprinkle with buttered bread crumbs and a light dusting of parmesan cheese. Bake at 350 degrees for 15 minutes, until thoroughly heated.

Try to serve 2 or 3 stuffed mushrooms, as a side dish, per person.

The Wild Game Hunter and His Cook

by
Robert F. Clark
(1970)

At this point in the production of this cookbook, the author and *my* cook thinks a few words on the care of big game, in the field, would be in order. I have strong feelings about this subject, and I hope this information can be brought to the hunter before the meat is brought to the cook.

Hunting antelope, deer, or elk in the Colorado mountains or plains is one of the finest recreations available to the man who still has the instinct for the hunt under his civilized skin. The thrill of stalking game in the beauty of autumn in the high country is made complete by the realization that you have provided your household with a goodly supply of delicious, tender meat for the table. The rules for keeping that meat sweet and tender are simple, and the process interesting, if not fun.

The first and most important step is bleeding and cooling the animal. A properly placed shot on an animal that doesn't suspect you are in the country and isn't running to get away from you, or some other hunter, is a great help in the work to come. I prefer a heart shot that only makes a couple of clean holes on each side of the rib cage but bleeds the animal out completely before he has gone fifty yards. A neck shot just ahead of the shoulder should be placed high enough to drop the animal in his tracks so that you can pull his head downhill and open the jugular vein immediately. On large animals such as elk or moose, use a big, heavy bullet at moderate speed. (I have seen the new Magnums ruin half an animal with a badly placed shot—where a heavier bullet with less velocity should hold together and do the job with little spoilage of meat.) A lighter, higher velocity bullet works well with deer and antelope, but if all you can see is the animal's rear end, don't shoot! There won't be anything left to eat.

Having bled the animal as well as possible under the circumstances, cut off his head. Pull his hind legs downhill and, starting at either end, slit the *skin only*, down the middle of the underside of the animal—from throat to tail and skin away from the slit, a few inches on each side, full length. (This can be done very rapidly if you have a hunting companion with you who will hold the animal in position. If you are alone, use the heavy twine or light rope you *always* carry with you to tie or prop him into position.) Now, cut through the breastbone, belly and pelvis, and after separating the diaphragm from the rib cage, just roll the whole entrails out—downhill, cutting around the anus just below the tail. Be sure to leave some evidence of sex attached to both hide and rear quarters to pass game warden inspection. (This tests your skinning ability—but it can be done!) Retrieve the heart and liver from the entrails, if you enjoy them. I think elk liver is a great delicacy, and we celebrate with a fresh liver dinner the day of the first kill. Do not soak the liver in water or do any unnecessary washing of it. Wipe it clean, after removing it from the attaching tissues, and lay it on a clean log or tuft of grass where the air can dry it while you are finishing the big job. I have a friend who pickles the heart and serves them for hors d' oeuvres. Very fine eating!

In passing, I may say that a friend who has been guiding in Wyoming for many years introduced me to a knife which is made in my own hometown of Boulder, Colorado. It makes the job easier and is easy to carry without weight or bulk and losability of the many fancier knives I have carried. It is a folding knife with one big blade that locks open and another 5-inch saw blade that is very sharp and makes the job of the breastbone and pelvis a snap on the heavier-boned animals.

Now, with the animal bled, field dressed, and propped open to cool (pull into the shade, if there is any)—comes the decision whether or not to skin at this point. I prefer to skin any animal at this stage, but if you are close to camp or it is getting dark or cold, it may be better to leave the hide on and drag the animal to camp or leave him propped open until morning. If he is a large animal and the weather is warm and it is early in the day, by all means, skin him immediately, right where he lies. Just roll him over on one side and skin—down to the backbone—then roll him back on his own hide and skin the other side. Slipping your knife in between the second and third rib forward of the loins, cut him in half. Cut the legs off in such a way as to leave the tendon properly connected to the joint so you can shove a stick through the natural loop formed there. It is simple when you know the feel of the joint, but if you don't—start below the joint and work up until you find it, or you'll lose your handles! Then, with a stout stick shoved between each pair of legs, you have two halves that you should be able to hang in the shady side of the nearest tree or clump of trees. If he's just too big to handle this way, you're stuck with quartering him, which requires a cut down the middle of the backbone—and this is the toughest job of all. However, once quartered and hung in the shade, you are assured of sweet meat regardless of the daytime temperature.

Regular game bags of cheese cloth or clean, old sheets brought from home can be used to keep flies off without stopping the cooling process and should be used immediately after the animal is cleaned, dressed, halved or quartered, as necessary. Cut dirty or blood-shot meat away and discard. Wipe out the intestinal and chest cavities with a clean dry rag (or a handful of aspen "quakie" leaves will do well), but *do not wash* with water unless "gut" shot, in which case, use water sparingly and dry thoroughly. The skin that forms as the meat dries is plenty of protection for ordinary dust and a few leaves or pine needles won't hurt the meat. If you have to leave your quarters hung at the scene overnight, you will be surprised how much lighter and easier to handle they will be the next day.

In case you have noticed an omission of my mentioning the scent glands here, I can only say that when I first started hunting in Colorado in 1946, I didn't now about them. After learning about them and fussing with them, a game warden came upon me one bright fall day while I was cutting the little tufts off the inside of the legs of a deer. He laughed, saying I was wasting my time—just be more careful about getting hair on the meat and forget the glands. His advice must have been good, as I've never bothered about them since and never could tell the difference. One thing that *does* make a *big* difference is trimming off as much of the fat as is possible, before wrapping him up. Game tallow is great for dressing leather, but it has no place in the cook pot!

To my mind, antelope are the hardest to handle on account of the hair. The hair is hollow and brittle and skinning the animal completely before dressing is usually the best answer. If you can find any shade at all, even the shade of your Jeep, or pickup truck, to lay him in after he's skinned and propped open, it is a great advantage. Usually there is enough breeze to cool the little animal fast, if you can just fine a bit of shade.

The last bit of advice I can give is on transportation. We always try to break camp early in the morning and by this time the carcasses should have hung and cooled for several days, or at least overnight. Fold a tent several times and lay the cold meat on the folded tent on the floor of a pickup or Jeep and then cover with another folded tent or tarp and insulate all around the edges with whatever you have—sleeping bags, more tents—anything so warm air does not get in. Shoving your hand into the pack even in late afternoon of a hot day should find the meat still cold to the touch and very firm. If not—stop, unpack, and cool.

The most sickening sight I have seen, and I saw it again just last fall, is a station wagon heading east on an interstate highway with two big, beautiful elk—the heads and hides still on, tied on the top rack—in the sun!! In this case there should be open season on the hunter—not the animal.

If any of you who read this happen to love hunting, but the wife says "don't bring that evil-smelling stuff home to me"—I hope the recipes in this book will put you back in the saddle again. I simply appreciate the effort my wife has made to make my hunting trips pay off—at the table!

Outdoor and Wild Game Cookery

Foreword

Of course, any of these recipes can be made in your own kitchen, but I actually hope to inspire you to the true adventure of taking to the great outdoors. Bundle up your camp gear, take along a couple heavy skillets, a big black Dutch oven, a lot of charcoal, the coffee pot, and your courage! Those of kindred spirit who go along with you won't mind taking a chance on what the cooks can come up with. Plan ahead—be inventive. If you didn't bring along quite the right thing—improvise! Time will improve your ability to put on a truly gourmet meal in the most primitive surroundings.

Have you ever known what it's like to wake to the crackle of the campfire and the wonderful smell of coffee beginning to cook? I think, "Goodness, I must have overslept—and it's my turn to get breakfast. There'll be homemade antelope sausage and sourdough pancakes with wild flower honey! (Make you hungry?) They'll all be up soon and table should be set—better warm the honey in a pan of hot water, too—makes it taste better!" As I hurriedly slip on my clothes I'm remembering, too, that lunches must be packed today—the men are heading for the beaver pond to fish, one of the girls wants to go up on the South Ridge to sketch the peak to the west—which, even now, is catching the first pink glow of day. (Who said I overslept? It's not even six o'clock yet—but they're all full of pep and anxious to get going for the day.) No matter! Bedtime comes early in the mountains after night time comes on. Night is a wonderful time in the mountains—so peaceful and quiet as you sit about the campfire with that last cup of coffee. Dinner was most satisfying—a huge Dutch oven filled with meat and vegetables in a luscious sauce—there was bannock cooked with a few raisins in it, and fresh watercress in the salad. One of the girls even brought pretty placemats for the plank table!

At night when quiet has come to the camp, only the rustle of the wind in the aspen leaves can be heard. In the far distance, the howl of a coyote—overhead and far away, the drone of a plane—the only reminder of our link with civilization. How sweet it is!

But—it doesn't have to end there. You can do it! Here, everything is right with the world. How rare! So—take along your cookbook and read awhile. Here's to happy times ahead!

WILD GAME & OUTDOOR COOKERY

Venison Pasties

A meat turnover that will please everyone—a meal in itself!

Prepare crust for a two-crust pie from your favorite recipe or use mine at the end of the pie chapter. Roll out half the dough and place in a 9-inch pie plate. Mix remaining ingredients in a large bowl or pan:

1 lb. venison, cut in little cubes (raw)
2 potatoes, diced
2 carrots, sliced thin
3 T. minced onion
1 t. salt
¼ t. dried sage
2 t. dried parsley
2 T. water
4 T. butter, melted

Toss well and put *half* the mixture on the pastry. Fold over in a half moon, filling one-half the pie plate. Crimp edges to seal—do not pierce or slit crust. Roll out remaining dough and repeat process. You will have 2 half-pies. Bake in medium preheated oven (350 degrees) for 1 hour and 10 minutes. Test by piercing crust with a sharp knife to make sure vegetables are tender.

Serves 4.

Note: This may be baked in a preheated camp dutch oven. Heat oven on a bed of coals until it sizzles. (Place a trivet in the bottom.) Put pie in—cover and put more coals on top to insure browning and even heating. Keep plenty of coals going to add as the first coals cool or burn out. Bake as directed.

Cowboy Stew

Perfect for a cold night—so easy!

In a heavy kettle (or dutch oven), over medium heat (campfire, charcoal, or at home), render the fat from four slices of bacon, diced. When bacon is nearly crisp, remove from pan and add 1 lb. or more of elk, deer, antelope, or beef. Cut in 1-inch cubes and sprinkle with 1 T. flour, ½ t. salt, and ¼ t. pepper. Brown well on all sides. Add 2 potatoes, cubed, and 1 large onion, diced. Stir well and allow onion to become limp but not browned. Add water or canned beef broth to barely cover. Simmer covered for 2 hours. Remove cover during last half hour and let liquid cook down.

Serves 4. Liquid may be thickened, if necessary.

Baked Colorado Trout With Bacon

Wash 4 fresh-caught trout, drain, and pat dry with paper toweling.

In a shallow baking pan, lay 8 slices of bacon and place the trout over the bacon. Sprinkle with ½ t. salt and ¼ t. pepper. Cover pan with foil, sealing edges tightly. Bake 20 to 25 minutes at 375 degrees, until the meat at the back will flake easily with a fork. With a long spatula, gently lift trout and bacon, which should be browned, to a warm platter. Garnish with parsley and lemon. This avoids having to turn trout—a somewhat difficult job at times.

Margaret Reedy's "Juniper Game Marinade"

Combine and let stand 2 weeks to develop full flavor:

3 qts. red wine
1 pt. red wine vinegar
½ C. whole black peppercorns
3 T. salt
1 t. minced fresh rosemary
3 bay leaves
½ C. minced dried onion
1 T. juniper berries
2 cloves garlic, pressed

At end of two weeks, strain and bottle. Makes 8 pts. of fine marinade for any game, including rabbit.

Venison Pot Roast De Luxe

Recipe may be used equally well with elk or beef.

Remove all fat from a large venison roast (6 to 8 lbs.) and sprinkle with salt and fresh ground pepper, rubbing it well into the meat.

In a large cast iron pot (dutch over, preferred), melt 4 T. butter over medium heat. Add the roast and turn frequently, until well browned. Chop 2 medium-sized onions and add to the roast, stirring well in the fat.

Add:
2½ C. hot water
2 bay leaves
1 clove garlic, pressed
¼ t. allspice
4 T. honey
4 fillets of anchovy mashed in:
2 T. vinegar
1 t. salt
Fresh ground pepper
3 carrots, cut in chunks

Stir thoroughly and bring to boiling point. Reduce heat. Simmer for 2½ hours. Remove roast to warm place. Strain the pan juices and return to the pot. Stir in 2 C. sour cream mixed with 4 T. flour. Allow to thicken, but do not boil rapidly (as the cream will separate). Return roast to the sauce and *simmer* for 10 minutes.

Serves 8 to 10.

Venison or Elk "Jumberjack"

Combine:

½ C. salad oil
Juice of 1 lemon
¼ t. freshly ground pepper
1 T. minced parsley
1 small bay leaf
1 clove garlic, pressed

Cut 6 ½-inch-thick slices from loin of venison (making 6 nice serving pieces). Pour the marinade over steaks and allow to stand 1 hour. Wipe steaks and broil on hot coals, basting with the marinade to desired doneness—3 minutes on each side is enough for game lovers! Serve with sauted fresh mushrooms and pass a dish of cream gravy.

Game and Noodles

In 3 T. butter, saute 1 lb. ground game meat (free of game fat) until lightly brown.

Add:
½ C. diced onion
¼ C. diced green pepper
½ C. sliced celery

Stir with meat for 5 minutes and add:

1 No. 2 can red kidney beans, drained
2 C. tomatoes
1 4-oz. can mushrooms and juice
2 C. broad noodles, precooked 10 min. and drained
1½ t. salt
1 t. chili powder
¼ t. pepper
8 green stuffed olives, sliced

Combine all ingredients and turn into a buttered 1½-qt. casserole. Sprinkle with buttered bread crumbs and bake at 350 degrees for 1 hour.

Serves 6.

Quail Pie

Coat 6 well-dressed quail with a mixture of 3 T. flour, ½ t. salt, and ⅛ t. pepper.

In a heavy skillet, melt ¼ C. butter and saute the quail to a golden brown. remove the quail to a 2-qt. baking dish. In the remaining butter, saute ½ lb. fresh mushrooms, ¼ C. diced green onions, and ½ C. diced celery, until vegetables are tender but not brown. Add ½ lb. cooked, diced ham and 2 C. chicken broth (canned is fine). Stir 2 T. flour into ¼ C. water and add to the simmering vegetables and broth. When it boils and thickens, add to the quail in the baking dish. Meanwhile, prepare dough for a single-crust pie (see pie chapter). Roll and fit to the baking dish. Flute edge and slash vents to allow steam to escape. Bake at 350 degrees for 50 minutes or until pastry is well browned!

Serves 6.

Roast Pheasant with Wild Rice

In a large saucepan, over hot fire, bring 3 C. water and 1 t. salt to a boil. Add 1 C. wild rice and allow to boil again. Reduce heat and simmer 40 minutes or until water is absorbed and rice is tender.

In a skillet, melt 4 T. butter and in it, saute ½ lb. fresh, sliced mushrooms and 2 T. green onion tops. Add ½ C. chopped pecans and add all to the rice. Cool.

Divide the rice mixture into the cavities for 2 dressed pheasants (about 2- or 3-lb. birds). Brush pheasants with melted butter and bake in an uncovered roasting pan at 350 degrees for 1 to 1½ hours (about 30 minutes per pound). Baste frequently with 1 C. dry white wine and 1/3 C. melted butter.

Serves 5 or 6.

Elk Sirloin Au Roquefort

Cut a large sirloin steak about 1½ inches thick. Mash 2 T. crumbled roquefort cheese and combine with 2 T. salad oil, 1 T. lemon juice, and fresh ground pepper. (Salt the steak after it comes to the table.) Spread the mixture on both sides of the steak. Allow to stand 1 hour or more.

Prepare the coals and grill steak 5 inches from the coals (medium rare will take 8 minutes per side). Turn once. Sprinkle top with additional roquefort, crumbled, and a bit of parsley, minced.

Serves 6.

Antelope Shishkebobs

A real delicacy.

Combine:

¼ C. pineapple juice

¼ C. honey

¼ C. salad oil

2 T. soy sauce

¼ C. chili sauce

Alternately space 1½-inch-thick squares of antelope round steak with pineapple chunks, cherry tomatoes, whole canned onions, pepper chunks, and whole canned mushrooms, on long metal skewers. Marinate several hours, turning frequently (a broiler pan makes a good pan for this!). Allow coals to burn down to white ashes. Cook shishkebobs to desired doneness, turning frequently—about 10 minutes in all. Sauce will marinate about 6 or 8 skewer-fulls.

A Tip On Cutting Game Steaks

When preparing for the freezer, always cut steaks extra thick—thin steaks get done too fast and dry out. If you want thinner steaks, they can be easily cut when partly thawed.

Corn On the Cob I

Remove heavy outer husks. Turn back husks and remove silks. Replace husks. Soak corn in a pail of water for 10 minutes. Drain and shake well. Place corn on grill, turning often, for 10 or 12 minutes. Peel off brown husks and serve corn with butter, salt, and pepper.

Corn on the Cob II

Remove husks and silk from as many ears of corn as you need. Prepare a square of foil for each that will completely envelop the ear. Place corn on square of foil and butter, completely, the raw corn—salt and pepper it also. Sprinkle each with a few drops of water. Roll up foil to seal. Place on grill and cook 8 to 12 minutes, turning frequently.

Prime Venison Chops

Have the venison chops cut at least ¾ inch thick. Trim off any fat and sprinkle meat with unseasoned tenderizer. Heat a heavy skillet until it sizzles. Add 3 T. butter and immediately add the chops. Cook 3 ro 4 minutes per side. Season with a hint of garlic salt and fresh ground pepper. Serve on hot platter and turn the pan juices over all. Squeeze over all the juice of ½ lemon. Serve with creamed potatoes and a big green salad!

Elk Burgundy

Combine:

2 lbs. ground elk meat
2 t. salt
½ t. pepper
½ t. thyme
½ C. chopped onion
½ C. milk
1 egg, beaten

Mix thoroughly and shape into 6 "steaks." Place each on a square of foil and seal into packets. Place on grill over glowing coals. Brown on both sides from 5 to 8 minutes.

Combine:
¼ c. burgundy wine
1/3 C. salad oil

Open packets and baste meat with the wine mixture for several minutes. Serve with a pan of fresh fried mushrooms—or onions!

Serves 6.

Squaw Corn

Dice 6 slices bacon and fry until crisp in a heavy skillet. Remove bacon and reserve. Remove all but 2 T. fat from pan and add ¼ C. diced onion and 2 T. green pepper, diced. Fry slowly until tender. Add 1 No. 2 can cream style corn to the pan and heat thoroughly. Break 4 eggs into a dish, but do not beat. Turn into the corn mixture and stir slowly until the mixture thickens and eggs are cooked. Season with a little salt and pepper.

Serves 6.

Dutch Meat Loaf

Combine:

1½ lbs. ground game meat
½ lb. pork sausage
¼ C. diced onion
2/3 C. tomato sauce
1 C. soft bread crumbs
1 egg, beaten
1½ t. salt
⅛ t. pepper

Mix well and shape into a loaf in a shallow baking pan. Bake in a 350-degree oven for 1½ hours.

Meanwhile, prepare the sauce of :

1/3 C. tomato sauce
½ C. water
2 T. brown sugar
1 T. mustard
1 T. vinegar

When sauce is mixed, turn over the meat loaf, spooning it up over the loaf occasionally as it bakes.

Bear Steak

You'll have a rare treat in store if you've never tasted bear meat—providing your hunter knows his business. Bear tastes like a cross between beef and pork—juices make delicious gravy. All bear fat must be removed. It is one of the most delicious (and rare) treats I've ever tasted! The meat should be cooked as any good piece of meat—but is best either *medium* or well done. Try it as a roast, cooking like a beef pot roast, with gravy, or try this:

Make a marinade for a 4- or 5-lb. slice of bear loin steak by combining:

2 C. claret wine
1 C. wine vinegar
1 bay leaf
2 T. dried parsley
½ t. thyme
1 T. salt
½ t. ground pepper
2 cloves garlic, pressed
1 medium onion, diced

Let steak marinade in this mixture for 24 hours. Remove from marinade and wipe with paper toweling. Grill over hot coals to medium (*barely* pink), basting with garlic butter (3 T. butter and 1 small clove garlic, pressed). When cooked to desired doneness, remove to a hot platter and dust lightly with salt and pepper. Wonderful served with Spanish Rice and Fresh Spinach Salad!

Potato Pancakes With Bratwurst

Grate 4 large potatoes and drain well in a collander (or press with fingers).

Add:
¾ C. flour
½ t. salt
3 eggs, unbeaten

Beat all together and fry in small cakes on hot, greased griddle. Meanwhile, heat to boiling 6 large bratwurst sausages. Drain and place on grill over white-ash coals. Turn frequently until crispy brown. Serve with potato pancakes and warm applesauce!

RECIPES FOR HEALTH & NUTRITION

Health Bread

In a large mixing bowl, stir together:

2 C. flour
1 C. whole wheat flour
2 pkgs. dry yeast

In another large bowl, combine:

1 C. quick-cooking oatmeal
1 C. whole bran cereal
1 C. raisins
2½ C. boiling water
2 T. shortening
2 t. salt
½ C. molasses
1½ C. cream style cottage cheese

Cook to lukewarm. Add to the first bowl of ingredients. Beat at low speed 3 minutes. By hand, stir in enough flour to make a moderately stiff dough. Knead on a floured surface 5 to 7 minutes or until smooth. Place in a greased bowl and allow to rise, double in bulk. Punch down. Shape into 3 loaves. Place in 3 8- x 4-inch loaf pans. Let raise to double. Bake at 375 degrees for 35 minutes or until brown. Cool on racks.

Makes 3 loaves.

Banana Wheat Pancakes

Makes about 12 6-inch pancakes.

Combine:

¾ C. whole wheat flour

¼ C. white or unbleached flour

1/3 C. All-Bran Cereal

2 t. baking powder

¼ t. salt

Add:

1¼ C. milk

2 T. salad oil

1 egg, slightly beaten

Stir in 1 medium banana, chopped fine. Bake on a hot, lightly greased griddle, turning once, using about ¼ C. batter per pancake.

Willie's Oven Pancakes

Set oven temperature to 450 degrees

In a heavy skillet (that can go into the oven), melt with the heat of the oven 3 T. margarine.

Beat 3 eggs until well mixed. Add:

½ C. flour
¼ t. salt
½ C. milk

Stir in melted margarine. Beat smooth and pour into hot skillet. Bake at 450 degrees for 15 minutes. Reduce heat to 350 degrees for 5 to 10 minutes or until puffed and brown. Sprinkle with juice from ½ lemon and a liberal dusting of powdered sugar.

Serves 2.

Wheat Germ Meatloaf

Combine:

1 lb. ground lean beef
½ lb. ground lean pork
½ C. cracker crumbs
½ C. wheat germ
1 beaten egg
½ C. milk
½ C. chopped onion
2/3 C. tomato catsup or tomato sauce
1 t. worcestershire sauce
½ t. salt
Dash of pepper
1 t. dried basil
1 T. romano cheese, grated

Combine all ingredients and spoon into a 9 x 5 x 3 inch loaf pan. Bake at 350 degrees for 50 to 55 minutes.

Serves 6 to 8.

Cottage Cheese Loaf

In a large mixing bowl, combine well:

2 C. cream style cottage cheese
1 large green pepper, minced
2 large carrots, grated
1 T. dehydrated instant minced onion
½ t. salt
2 C. fine dry bread crumbs
2 eggs, well beaten
¼ C. milk

Oil an 8- x 4-inch loaf pan and line with waxed paper. Oil paper. Place mixture *firmly* in pan. Bake at 350 degrees for 35 to 40 minutes. Invert on serving dish and peel off paper. Serve with mushroom sauce, if desired.

Serves 4 to 6.

Curried Chicken Souffle

Saute 2 T. minced onion in ¼ C. margarine. Remove from heat and add, stirring well:

½ t. curry powder
1/3 C. flour

Gradually add:
1 10½-oz. can chicken broth or 1¼ C. homemade stock
¼ t. salt
Dash of pepper
¼ C. green pepper, minced
1½ C. cooked chicken, minced

Cook 5 minutes; cool 5 minutes. Blend in 1 C. Egg Beaters (egg substitute), thawed. Beat 3 eggwhites until stiff and fold into the chicken mixture, 1/3 at a time. Pour into a well-oiled, 2-qt. souffle dish which has been sprinkled with about ¼ C. dry bread crumbs. Bake at 375 degrees for 55 minutes. Serve at once.

Serves 6.

Broccoli Walnut Casserole

Cook ¾ C. brown rice according to package directions. Lightly brown 1 C. walnuts, chopped coarsely in 3 T. vegetable oil. Remove walnuts and set aside. To the oil, add:

½ C. green onion, including tops
½ lb. fresh mushrooms, sliced
1 clove garlic, minced
3 C. broccoli, stems sliced thin and the head separated into flowerettes

Stir fry until broccoli is tender-crisp. Add:

½ C. sour cream
1 T. light soy sauce

Toss well. Add the precooked rice and walnuts. Turn into a 2-qt. casserole. Sprinkle with about 1 C. grated cheddar cheese. Bake at 375 degrees about 30 minutes.

Seves 4 to 6.

Lemon-Dill Fish Fillets

In a shallow baking dish, place 4 fish fillets (halibut, perch, or red snapper). Lightly salt the fillets. Sprinkle each fillet with a mixture of:

1 small onion, minced
1 t. dill weed
½ t. paprika
2 T. fresh parsley, minced

Over all, squeeze the juice of 1 lemon. Cover and bake at 350 degrees for 25 minutes. Uncover and bake 5 minutes more.

Serves 4.

Tofu With Eggs & Vegies

Melt 1 T. margarine in a 10-inch skillet. Add 1 C. tofu (mashed), saute over medium heat until light brown. Add 2 eggs, slightly beaten. Season lightly with salt and pepper. Add any of the following vegies: chives, bean or alfalfa sprouts, crushed garlic, mushrooms, green onions, or green pepper, minced. Season lightly with soy sauce. If mixture seems dry, add one egg, slightly beaten, *after* removing from heat. Stir well.

Serves 2 or 3.

Chinese Cabbage Sprout Salad

In a jar, combine and shake well:

¼ C. red wine vinegar
3 T. safflower oil
2 t. sesame oil
¼ t. salt
1 t. dry mustard
1 T. sugar

In a serving bowl, combine:

2 C. fresh bean sprouts
½ C. raw mushrooms, sliced
2 C. Chinese cabbage, shredded
1 cucumber, peeled and thinly sliced

Toss with above dressing. Chill.

Serves 4.

Chicken Salad In Pita Bread

Four pita bread rounds, with slice removed from one side to form a pocket. Toast if desired.

Filling:

1½ C. thinly sliced, cooked chicken
1 T. minced green onion
½ t. fresh or dried dill weed
1 C. alfalfa sprouts
1/3 C. thinly sliced radishes
½ C. celery, thinly sliced

In a small bowl, combine:
½ C. plain yogurt
¼ C. low-fat mayonnaise
½ t. salt
Dash of pepper

Lightly combine dressing and chicken-vegetable mixture and fill pita rounds. Garnish with sliced tomatoes and parsley sprigs.

Serves 4.

Mock Mayonnaise

In a blender, combine:

1 C. cottage cheese
2 T. salad oil
1 T. cider vinegar
2 t. sugar
¼ t. salt
½ t. dry mustard
½ t. paprika
Dash pepper

Process until smooth, scraping from sides into blades with a rubber spatula several times. Cover. Refrigerate. Use within two weeks.

Yield: 1 1/3 cups.

Buttermilk Lo-Cal Dressing

In a small jar, shake together vigorously:

½ C. buttermilk (thick)
1 t. red wine vinegar
1 t. sugar
½ T. lemon juice
Fresh or dried basil leaves to taste
Salt and pepper to taste

Yield: ½ cup.

Grape Whip

Dissolve 1 pkg. (3-oz.) grape low-cal gelatin in 1 C. boiling water. Stir until dissolved. Chill until the gelatin *starts* to thicken. Add 1 8-oz. container plain yogurt. Beat at high speed until light and fluffy. Chill briefly until mixture rounds up on a spoon.

Serve in four small glass dishes. Serves 4. Other flavors of gelatin may be used.

Granola Candy Bars

Great for a hunting trip!

In a 3-qt. saucepan, melt ¾ C. butter or margarine over low heat. Add, stirring until well blended:

½ C. brown sugar
½ C. honey
1 t. vanilla
¼ t. salt

Stir in:
4½ C. granola style cereal
2/3 C. chopped nuts, coconut, or sunflower seeds

Turn into a well-greased 10- x 15-inch pan. Press down firmly. Bake at 375 degrees for 15 to 20 minutes. Cool. Cut into 32 bars. If preparing for camping, hunting, etc., wrap bars in squares of plastic wrap.

Carrot Meatloaf

Combine:

1 lb. lean ground beef
2 large carrots, grated
1 medium onion, chopped
½ C. cornflake crumbs
½ C. skim milk
1 egg
1 t. worcestershire sauce
1 t. salt (or less)
¼ t. pepper

Spoon into a 8 x 4 x 3 inch loaf pan. Bake at 350 degrees for 1 hour. Let stand 10 minutes before serving.

No-Oil Herb Salad Dressing

Whirl in a blender until well combined:

1¼ C. no-salt tomato juice
1 t. dehydrated instant onion flakes
1 T. Dijon mustard
2 t. chopped fresh dill or 1 t. dry dill weed
¼ t. freshly ground pepper
⅛ t. salt

Salt may be omitted for those on salt-free diets and is still a delicious dressing!

Dear Friends:

Do enjoy this little cookbook! I hope it will bring you many happy hours of preparation, cooking, and eating!

Good luck.

Your friend,

Sara M. Clark

Index